Pricing

Pricing

RUSSELL S. WINER

MARKETING SCIENCE INSTITUTE

Cambridge, Massachusetts

Contents

Foreword

It is our pleasure to present *Pricing* by Russell Winer, the fourth book in the MSI Relevant Knowledge Series. Management surveys across the continents continue to list pricing as the #1 strategic issue for marketing decision makers. A major reason for this sustained interest is that competitive pricing behaviors—and customers' reactions—have undergone so much change of late, due in part to the Internet, to new opportunities for outsourcing, and to currency redefinitions.

Russ Winer is a world-class expert in this field, and his monograph reviews the major aspects of pricing in concise and managerial terms. He presents both the psychological and the economic dimensions of pricing, a rare combination in one volume. His inferences are based on scholarly research, including "classic" contributions to pricing as well as recent developments. He also includes important coverage of pricing issues that are paramount to services marketing in the Internet age, in particular, Internet auctions and yield management.

Pricing follows *Sales Promotion* by Scott Neslin, *Branding and Brand Equity* by Kevin Lane Keller, and *Service Quality* by Valarie Zeithaml and A. Parasuraman. I am confident that *Pricing*, like its predecessors, will become a much-consulted reference for the MSI audience.

> *Dominique M. Hanssens*
> *UCLA*
> *MSI Executive Director 2005–07*

ACKNOWLEDGEMENTS

This is an expanded version of a chapter published in the 2002 *Handbook of Marketing* edited by Barton Weitz and Robin Wensley, published by Sage Publications. I would like to thank my co-author on that chapter, Professor Chezy Ofir of the Hebrew University of Jerusalem, for stimulating many of the ideas represented in this monograph. I also appreciate comments made by my New York University colleague, Yuxin Chen. I thank Annie Law for research assistance.

Russell S. Winer
New York University

Executive Summary

Pricing is often thought to be the most important decision under a marketing manager's control. As an observable "component" of a product or service, price results in customer purchase or nonpurchase. It simultaneously affects the profit margin per unit sold. Price is also a communications decision, signaling to the customer the value and quality of the product or service relative to competitors.

The managerial pricing decision has four components: (1) cost structure, (2) competitors' prices, (3) the value the customer places on the brand versus its competitors, and (4) marketing strategy. Research on pricing draws on both the economics and psychology literature; this monograph addresses six major areas of study.

Customer Value: Measurement and Scaling Issues

Customer value (also called willingness-to-pay or reservation price) is a key element in the price-setting decision. Two sources of data are used to estimate customer value: actual transactions data and survey data.

Transactions data are readily available and allow the firm to estimate customer value by calculating customers' price elasticity. However, transactions data are limited to the highest price in the product category; they do not disclose whether a customer would pay a price higher than that offered in the market.

Survey data are used to estimate customer value through direct questioning that elicits customers' price thresholds. Early research assumed an inverted U-shaped consumer response function; direct questions forced consumers to associate low price with low quality and to view high prices as too expensive. More recent research on the lower threshold demonstrates two consumer functions, reflecting different price perceptions and acceptability judgments: (1) a "cheaper the better" reaction suggested by economic theory, and (2) a "low price = low quality" reaction suggested by the early marketing literature.

Behavioral Response to Price

Consumers are active processors of price information. Thus, the psychological literature develops a number of key concepts regarding consumer response to price.

Price Knowledge and Judgments   Price recall studies suggest that consumers do not pay attention to the prices they pay. Other research finds that a simple task characteristic may have significantly biased this finding. Further, in studies that tap long-term memory, researchers find that while customers may not recall exact prices, they possess a working knowledge of prices that is sufficiently accurate for good decisionmaking. Finally, the competitive environment is shown to affect consumer price judgments.

"Odd" Pricing   Certain price endings (0, 5, 9) occur much more frequently than others; research interest has focused in particular on 9 endings, often called "odd" or "just below" prices. To explain the frequent use of odd prices, academics have proposed that consumers do not process price holistically but, instead, use some heuristic to process the digits separately.

Reference Prices   A reference price is any standard of comparison against which an observed price is compared. External reference prices are usually observed prices (e.g., the "regular retail price"). Internal reference prices are mental prices used to assess an actual price observed in the marketplace.

Internal reference prices have a strong effect on buying behavior. When the observed price is higher than the reference price, it can negatively affect purchasing because the consumer perceives this as an unpleasant surprise or a bad deal.

Another component of reference price is expected future price; this concept is particularly important for any product category (such as new consumer durables) that experiences significant price changes over time.

Fairness Perceptions of price unfairness can have a significant negative impact on a firm, including consumers not purchasing, spreading negative word-of-mouth, and engaging in other negative actions. Research finds two main sources of perceived unfairness: (1) the perceived profit being made by the vendor (excess profits) and (2) customers' inferences about the motives for the price perceived to be unfair (e.g., price gouging).

Experiments show that respondents consistently believe that selling prices are higher than fair prices. Further, consumers systematically underestimate the impact of inflation on prices. Price differences are perceived to be the fairest when they can be attributed to differences in quality.

Price/Quality When price is used to signal high quality, a higher price can sometimes lead to higher rather than lower demand. This usually occurs when a product's quality is difficult to assess before purchasing or difficult to assess at all.

Recent work has focused on mediating factors that might attenuate the relationship between price and perceived quality (e.g., the quantity of information presented to respondents).

Purchasing Context Effects Research finds that customer decision-making can vary greatly in different purchasing contexts. One study finds, for example, that a product's value to a customer can be enhanced by introducing a more expensive product in the purchasing context.

Pricing Tactics

Managers use a variety of pricing tactics in the pricing decision. A well-researched strategy is *bundling*, where complementary items are priced as a unit (e.g., McDonald's no. 1 meal). Price bundling may be an optimal strategy since the seller can extract a surplus from a customer who pays a price higher than his or her willingness-to-pay for one or more individual items to get other items in the bundle.

Bundling may also increase purchase likelihood for any one item since the utility for the bundle may be greater than the sum of the individual product utilities. An interesting situation arises when a service (such as a theater subscription) is bundled; research shows that customers are more likely to forgo consumption (and demand less compensation) for an individual benefit that is bought in a bundle.

In *unbundling*, a product or service comprises two prices (e.g., a cellular phone monthly access fee and usage charge). Other unbundling strategies are framing a price in smaller increments and partitioning prices (e.g., separate shipping and handling costs).

While economic theory suggests that consumers would prefer a special, bundled price, some results from psychology show that unbundled prices can result in higher overall product evaluations and greater choice.

Other pricing tactics include *flat-rate* and *single-usage fees*. AOL, for example, has moved from an access fee usage plan to a monthly flat rate with unlimited usage. Numerous empirical studies show that consumers systematically overestimate their usage of such services, incorrectly choosing a flat rate over a per-use rate.

Price-matching guarantees and *refunds* are usually communicated as part of store policy. Although economic theory predicts that prices are higher when such price-matching policies exist, retailers widely believe that price-matching policies actually instigate price competition (price wars) and can lead to lower prices.

Some pricing strategies are based on *consumer currency effects*. For example, based on the knowledge that consumers treat coins differently than paper money, new technology at some fast-food restaurants encourages consumers to spend the spare change they are about to receive on another, specially-priced, food item. Other research looks at how consumers value their own versus foreign currencies, and how companies might combine currencies (e.g., airlines charging a combination of frequent-flier miles and money for a plane ticket).

Two characteristics unique to services—perishability (e.g., an unfilled theater seat is lost revenue) and capacity constraint (there are a limited number of seats in a theater)—have resulted in *yield management* strategies. Research has offered algorithms for optimal pricing under these conditions. For example, one study shows that the services for which price-sensitive consumers make early purchases (i.e., airlines and hotels) are most suited to yield management strategies.

Empirical Research on Price

Price response—in the form of elasticities or other measures—has been the focus of a considerable amount of empirical research. A meta-analysis of 10 years' research shows that average price elasticity is about eight times larger (in absolute value) than advertising elasticity. Recent topics of interest include the following:

Interaction of Advertising and Price   Does advertising increase brand loyalty and product differentiation, and thus lower price elasticity? Or does it increase consideration sets and competition and thus raise price elasticity? Research finds support for both viewpoints and suggests that the type of advertising determines the effect: price-oriented advertising leads to greater price sensitivity, while advertising that is not price oriented has the reverse effect.

A study of the advertising-promotion interaction finds that although advertising and promotion have separate, positive effects on brand choice probabilities, sales promotion, being price-focused, has negative interaction with advertising. This finding has significant implications for optimal marketing spending.

Retailing Issues   Using widely available electronic scanner data, researchers have focused on the retailer's pricing problem. Research demonstrates support for the micromarketing concept (product assortments customized to the local clientele). Other studies using scanner data examine types of store promotions (off-the-shelf price discount versus in-store coupons) and the factors that affect retailer pricing behavior.

Pricing Decision Support Systems   The development of new technologies and the availability of real-time information on store sales by stockkeeping unit have provided the basis for pricing decision support systems that make possible rapid pricing updates.

Price Search   Prior work on price search has relied on Stigler's search theory (1961): people will search for price information to the point where the marginal benefits from search equal the marginal costs. More recent research finds that two other factors—habit and noneconomic returns such as shopping enjoyment—explain price search behavior better than economic returns.

Methodological Advances A considerable amount of effort in the pricing area has been devoted to improving methods for estimating price elasticities. The introduction of new statistical methodologies has benefited researchers and managers.

Game-Theoretic Models

Game theory is commonly used to examine the role of price as a coordination mechanism in the manufacturer/retailer channel. It is also used to model how supermarkets compete using different pricing formats and to model bargaining and power among channel members. In product policy research, game theory is used to model product differentiation, pricing for products that have branded components, and optimal pricing policies for new product introductions.

Pricing and the Internet

The rapid growth of the Internet as a distribution and information channel has spawned research on pricing issues in this context. With lower search costs, price competition on the Web is intensified, and pressure to differentiate on nonprice dimensions is increased.

Dynamic Pricing The Web enables firms to target customers more effectively and to price-discriminate. Some sites offer different prices to different shoppers at the same site for the same product depending upon the shoppers' past history, the prices of the products being examined, and the sites from which they came. For example, if a customer visits a site and does a price comparison, a site may automatically adjust its prices to the lowest price as it senses that the customer is price elastic. This type of dynamic pricing, while it has the potential to optimize profits, raises interesting issues regarding brand equity and the ethical dimensions of price discrimination.

Pricing Mechanisms Retail websites that offer *set prices* for products are most heavily affected by the Web's price-comparison capabilities; such sites must either match the lower prices or differentiate themselves on another dimension. Real-time *buyer/seller negotiations* emerged during the Internet boom period; although they have disappeared, these remain an interesting topic for future research. In *exchanges*, a group of buyers and sellers interact in electronic marketplaces to trade and set prices for transactions. Also emerging on the Internet are *micropayments* for an increment of Internet content (e.g., one song from iTunes).

Online auctions, in which competition among buyers and/or sellers results in prices that vary widely across transactions, are one of the most popular innovations of the Internet. In the classic English auction model, competition among buyers leads to a price. eBay offers this kind of system. In a reverse auction, sellers compete for a buyer's business. Some general findings are as follows: auctions are characterized by information asymmetries (e.g., the seller has more information than the buyer). Due to this asymmetry, there is a significant possibility that the winner will overpay as bidders tend to overvalue the item. In addition, ascending auctions are the most popular format, and in most Internet auctions, bids occur in the last few seconds of auctions lasting days or weeks.

Price Search Behavior Research has examined the efficiency of the online versus offline environment in terms of price levels, price elasticity, menu costs, and price dispersion. The empirical research on comparative *price levels* between online and offline retailing is mixed and limited to a few product categories.

Some studies have found that *price elasticities* on the Web are quite large. Other research has found that lowering the search costs for quality for differentiated products (e.g., wine) decreases price. One study shows that for electronics products, price elasticities can be very large when shopbots are used to conduct the search. Another study finds that customers do not really search that much on the Web. Thus, it is possible that online price sensitivity could ultimately be lower than offline.

Research finds that *menu costs* on the Internet are lower than in offline retailing, in that Internet merchants make significantly more price changes than their offline counterparts. Finally, a survey of a number of empirical studies concludes there is substantial *price dispersion* on the Internet, and there is no evidence that there is less price variation on the Internet than in offline environments. In addition, a longitudinal analysis showed that while the dispersion on the Internet has declined slightly over time, it is still substantial.

Introduction

It is generally asserted that the most important marketing decision under the control of management is price. The price a firm can charge for its product or service is determined by four factors: (1) cost structure, (2) competitors' prices, (3) the value the customer places on the brand versus its competitors, and (4) marketing strategy. These factors are dynamic, and price is often adjusted in response. In addition, price is an important communications tool that signals quality, discounting, and relative value compared to a competitor's offering. Therefore, the price decision is affected by economic forces, by management's understanding of consumer response, and by the firm's marketing strategy. Not surprisingly, as a result, the academic literature on pricing is based largely on both economic and psychological theories.

The purpose of this monograph is to review the academic literature on pricing, particularly that of the last decade. I will focus on six areas of research. First, I will cover the measurement and scaling of customer value, a central concept to pricing. Next, I will review the literature on customer response to pricing, as well as research on the wide variety of pricing tactics. There is a large empirical literature on pricing, particularly that using electronic scanner panel data from retail stores. I will review the substantive and methodological contributions of this work, as well as discuss competitive models, particularly game-theoretic models. Finally, I will review the large emerging literature on the implications of the Internet for pricing. I will conclude with some future directions for pricing research.

Russell S. Winer

Pricing

The Pricing Decision

Pricing is the only managerial decision that directly affects revenues. While other decisions regarding variables such as advertising and channels of distribution impact a brand's performance, no other decision so directly impacts the customer and the bottom line. Price is an observable component of the product that results in customer purchase or nonpurchase and determines the profit margin per unit sold.

Price is also a communications decision, signaling to the customer the value and quality of the product relative to competing products. Customers interpret price the way they interpret advertisements. A price set higher than a competitor's conveys to the customer that the firm feels the brand delivers greater value. A price set at $3.99 may be interpreted differently than a price set at $4.00. A brand positioned as a luxury or high-quality brand but priced lower than expected may confuse the customer by diluting the image.

The pricing decision has four major components:

1. Cost structure. The pricing decision is often viewed as a way of recovering costs in that the price of a product or service must be higher than the cost of making or delivering it. Many companies calculate their unit costs (this is more difficult for services) and add a standard markup to obtain a target return on investment. This strategy is common in retailing : the store manager simply adds a margin to the cost from the supplier. However, while the price must be higher than the cost, a price derived in this manner may not represent what customers are willing to pay. Customers may be willing to pay more for the product or service, thus creating an opportunity cost for the company. Alternatively, customers may not be willing to pay the cost-driven price, eventually resulting in a downward price adjustment.

2. Competition. In practice, costs plus the competition, only two of the four factors, are commonly used together to set price. Managers use

competitors' prices as benchmarks. In the consumer product arena, for example, if the manager feels that the brand delivers more value than the nearest competitor, he or she may be motivated to set the price higher than the competitor by a certain amount. In industrial product categories, a manager may feel that the product is supported by better service or has superior durability relative to a competing product. Again, this is used to justify a higher price.

3. Customer value. Customer or perceived value is a measure of how much a customer is willing to pay for a product or service. Economists call this the reservation price: the most someone is willing to pay for a product (or the price at which the product is eliminated from the customer's budget). It is also called willingness-to-pay. Every customer has a psychological concept of such a price: they compare price information with the perceived value or benefits they would derive from the product. As customers assess price information, their sense of customer value is always formed relative to competitors' products. Although the absolute level of perceived value for a brand is important in its own right, relative customer value (that is, how customers value the product or service in terms of competing options) is used in the price-setting context.

4. Marketing strategy. The marketing strategy for a product—that is, its target market, positioning, and value proposition—is normally determined before price is set, so the price decision must be consistent with the strategy. The target market decision will determine whether and how prices vary over segments due to price discrimination—see, for example, Neslin (2002). In addition, brand positioning relative to competitors (e.g., high-end positioning) has implications for price.

This book covers academic research related to these four components. The research is categorized into six areas: the first two relate to the customer value component of the pricing decision. The remaining four relate to the cost structure, competition, and marketing strategy components of the pricing decision.

Customer Value: Measurement and Scaling Issues   As noted above, an important basic question in pricing is, How do we measure perceived customer value, willingness-to-pay, and other related concepts? Since the pioneering work of British researchers Gabor and Granger in the 1950s on price awareness and willingness-to-pay, researchers have developed sophisticated approaches to price response measurement, such as price thresholds, to the problem of price response measurement.

Behavioral Response to Price The classic approach to pricing is based on microeconomic principles; economists have been interested for centuries in how price matches supply and demand. Only relatively recently have academic researchers looked to psychology, which views customers not simply as price takers but as active processors of price information.

Pricing Tactics There are many variations of price, which further complicates the pricing decision. In bundling, for example, complementary products (e.g., a razor and blades) are offered at a special price. Products and services may also be unbundled (e.g., an air compressor and service contract). A newer pricing tactic is the use of micropayments for a unit of a product (e.g., one song from a CD for $.99 on iTunes). I will cover a number of such pricing tactics. For a discussion of price promotions, which this book will not cover, see Neslin (2002).

Empirical Research on Price A considerable amount of empirical research has focused on price; much has used secondary data such as electronic scanner panel data (or its predecessor, diary panel data). The resulting introduction of new statistical methodologies has benefited researchers and managers.

Game-Theoretic Models Game theory has rapidly diffused into marketing over the last 10–15 years. Although theoretical in nature, this work is a welcome addition to the literature since it incorporates competition into pricing models. A particular focus has been on channels of distribution and product policy.

Pricing and the Internet The rapid growth of the Internet as a distribution and information channel has spawned research on pricing issues in this context. With fixed prices rapidly disappearing in the face of auctions, opportunities for price personalization, and the widespread availability of price-comparison Web services, a very interesting new avenue for research has opened up.

Customer Value: Measurement and Scaling Issues

A key element in setting price is the manager's estimate of customer value (CV).[1] Figure 1 uses one product and one competitor to show the role customer value plays in the pricing decision. The "floor," or lowest price that a firm will usually charge, is cost.[2] The maximum that can be charged is the customer's value for the brand (or willingness-to-pay, or reservation price).[3] This maximum is the upper bound or threshold on price. The competing brand's CV is included here to emphasize the importance of understanding your brand's CV relative to the competition. The difference between customer value and cost is the strategic pric-

Figure 1
The Strategic Pricing Gap

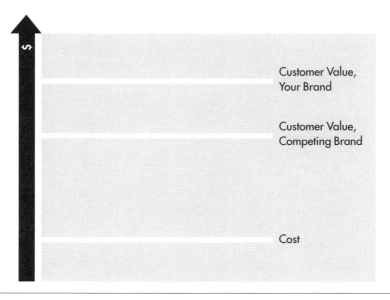

Figure 2
Pricing Scenarios

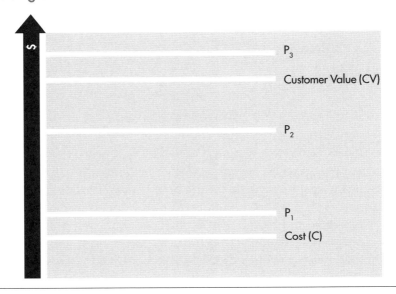

P_3

Customer Value (CV)

P_2

P_1

Cost (C)

ing gap. To understand how much latitude exists in the pricing decision, that is, to obtain this strategic pricing gap, the marketing manager must understand customer value.

Further, the manager must make informed decisions about how much of the pricing gap to concede to customers and how much to the company. This strategic decision is affected by a number of factors, including the competitors' prices, the marketing strategy, and so on. Figure 2 presents alternative pricing scenarios (ignoring competition). At price P_1, the company is making $P_1 - C$ as a margin and giving the customer $CV - P_1$ as a bonus or, in economic terms, as a surplus. At price P_2, the surplus $CV - P_2$ is much smaller. At P_3, very little sales will be produced (assuming that CV is a mean value with a distribution around it), which will quickly result in a downward adjustment in price.

Given this framework, it is clear that the question of how to measure customer value is critical. Of the two pricing errors, pricing too high or pricing too low, the latter is more significant in the long term. If a manager prices too high—above many customers' reservation prices—it will quickly become apparent in the marketplace, and price can be adjusted downward. However, if the price is set too low, money is "left on the table." Unnecessary price cuts are extremely expensive. Based on a 1992 survey, McKinsey & Co. estimated that the percentage decrease in profits from a 1% decrease in price range from a high of 23.7% in food and drug stores to a low of 2.4% in diversified financial services.

Two sources of data are used to estimate customer value: actual transactions data and survey data.

Transactions Data

Today, transaction data are readily available, particularly from grocery, drug, and discount stores at the retail level, and from services such as credit cards and telecommunications. Information about an individual household's (or business customer's) purchase history can be used to obtain CV. These data include information on the brand and quantity purchased, price paid, date, store, and many other measures.

One approach to understanding customer value is to estimate the customer's (or segment's) price elasticity from these transactions data. The concept of price elasticity of demand (E) can be expressed by the following equation:

$$E = \% \text{ change in demand} / \% \text{ change in price}.$$

Except in rare circumstances, E is normally negative; that is, a positive change in price results in a negative change in demand. At the individual-customer level, given sufficient observations or purchase occasions, E can be estimated using a demand model of the form

$$\ln Q = f(\ln P, \text{ other variables}),$$

where Q is the purchase quantity on an occasion, P is the price paid, and ln is the natural logarithm. In this model, the coefficient on $\ln P$ is an estimate of the customer's price elasticity.

A customer-level estimate of elasticity gives the manager a qualitative sense of CV (not a point estimate). The greater the price elasticity, the closer the customer is to CV, that is, to the maximum he or she is willing to pay for the product or service. There is little room to raise price for a price-elastic customer. Price inelasticity implies that there *is* room for the company to raise its price (although we do not know by how much).

A simpler approach is to examine the distribution of prices paid by the household. The highest price paid is an estimate of the CV or reservation price; the greater the number of purchase occasions, the more accurate the estimate.

A significant limitation is that a CV estimated from transactions data is limited to the highest price in the product category. Transactions data do not disclose whether a customer would pay a price higher than those offered in the market. In addition, this approach is not useful for new products for which transactions data are unavailable.

Survey Data

Direct Questioning   Surveys or experimental designs are used to estimate CV through direct questioning that elicits minimum and maximum price thresholds. Stoetzel, Sauerwein, and Vulpian (1954) criticized economic theory for its assumptions regarding prices and highlighted psychological aspects of price. They introduced a simple and easily implemented procedure whereby consumers are asked to indicate minimum and maximum prices for a product, as follows: "Below what price would you suspect that [a product] was of poor quality?" "Above what price would you judge [a product] to be too dear?" (see also Stoetzel 1970, p. 72). They conclude that consumers possess two thresholds and an acceptable range of prices between the thresholds.

Similarly, Adam (1958) investigates price perception and the effects of historical pricing on consumer perceptions and demand. In several studies he uses the direct questions Stoetzel and his colleagues formulated to suggest to consumers the existence of a price acceptability range with upper and lower thresholds. Following Stoetzel, Sauerwein, and Vulpian (1954) and Adam (1958), Fouilhé (1960) further investigates the methodology of direct questions regarding price thresholds. His results reconfirm the existence of minimum and maximum thresholds but indicate some empirical problems with the lower price thresholds and the distributional assumptions suggested by Adam (1958).

Stimulated by early work of the French researchers, Gabor and Granger (1961, 1966) further advance the idea of lower and upper price thresholds and the resultant price acceptability range. They assume three types of consumer responses to prices: too expensive, too cheap, and acceptable (price). Their work develops the distributional assumptions suggested by Adam (1958) and tests them empirically. Gabor and Granger (1966) also compare various measures of direct questions and obtain results similar to Adam's, leading Marbeau (1987) to conclude that the two direct questions suggested by Stoetzel are superior and simple to implement.

An extension of these measurement procedures is the Price Sensitivity Meter method (Van Westendorp 1976; for discussion see Monroe [1990]). This procedure presents different positions along a price acceptability continuum ranging from unacceptable price—cheap ("At what price would you consider this [product/brand] to be so inexpensive that you would have doubts about its quality?") to unacceptable price—too expensive ("...that the product is so expensive that regardless of its quality it is not worth buying?") (Monroe 1990, p. 114).

All of the methods described above assume that consumer response to price is represented by an inverted-U-shaped function. Hence, the direct questions force respondents to associate low prices with low quality and to view high prices as too expensive. However, this assumption may not apply to all products and consumers. For example, low prices may be quite acceptable and highly attractive in some contexts, and high prices may signal prestige. If so, the methods and measurement procedures discussed above are inherently biased.

To empirically assess the existence of a potential bias, Ofir, Bechtel, and Winer (2000) administer two measurement procedures to relatively low-income and below-average-income consumers. In the first procedure, consumers are presented a list of 10 prices for each of a number of products, and are asked to indicate the price acceptability for each on a seven-point scale. As expected, a substantial proportion of low-income consumers find low prices more acceptable (in line with economic theory). Separated by several unrelated tasks, consumers are asked to respond to Price Sensitivity Meter questions, which directly assess thresholds. Of those consumers who find low prices to be more acceptable in the first task, a substantial portion respond to the Price Sensitivity Meter as if they possess a lower price threshold (that is, lower prices mean poor quality), presumably because they are biased by the direct questions regarding thresholds. Specifically, 74–81.3% of low-income consumers have no problem with low prices of rice, jam, flour, and body lotion, but of those, 72.5–80% are biased by direct questions to indicate a lower threshold. These results provide clear evidence that direct questions regarding thresholds bias results. Specifically, it is most likely that there are consumers who prefer cheaper products. The implications for these consumers is that they only have an upper threshold (the reservation price) and not a lower threshold as well.

An interesting approach to measure thresholds and obtain the relevant price ranges is suggested by Monroe (1971a, b). Consumers are given a list of prices that they classify into categories using labels for each category (i.e., acceptable prices, etc.). The use of category labels associated with various acceptability levels provides an unbiased method to obtain consumer reactions to price. In Monroe (1971a), labels did not direct consumers in any way and thus were likely to be unbiased. In his recent discussion of this method, however, Monroe (1990) presented a mail survey version used in industry that is potentially biased by directing consumers to labels such as "unacceptable—too expensive" (p. 120).

Paired Comparisons Over the last five decades, researchers have observed that price judgments are inherently comparative (e.g., Scitovsky 1944–45; Emery 1970; Monroe 1990). Thus, paired-comparison tasks in which pairs of prices are graded on which price is more acceptable are assumed to be a natural task for consumers and may offer an unbiased way to research consumer reactions to price. Overall, the results among hundreds of consumers are very consistent, transitive, and reliable. Moreover, in this research two functions are observed, each reflecting different price perception and acceptability judgments. One is the "cheaper the better" reaction suggested by economic theory, and other exhibits an inverted-U-shaped function—the "low price = low quality" reaction suggested by the marketing literature.

Ofir (2004) tests the notion that customers possess two price acceptability functions, the standard downward-sloping demand curve and the inverted-U-shaped function. He uses a paired-comparison approach in which respondents must decide which of two prices is more acceptable and then rate how much more on a six-point scale anchored by zero (equal price acceptability). The results from 66 paired comparisons are analyzed using a well-known scaling approach (Wallsten et al. 1986), producing individual-level curves representing the acceptability of the alternative prices presented.

The results again demonstrate that both reactions to price (i.e., "cheaper is better" and "low price = low quality") exist. Moreover, the cumulative results suggest that the paired-comparisons method produces reliable and valid price scales.

Ofir (2004) also examines the effects of income and involvement with the product category on the shape of each function. Ofir posits that higher-income consumers, being less sensitive to price, less price conscious, and more engaged in price-quality inference than low-income consumers, will tend to perceive low prices as an indication of low quality and, therefore, will be more likely to react to price acceptability in a manner represented by an inverted-U-shaped function. He also postulates that involved customers are more concerned with the benefits of the product than its price. He hypothesizes, therefore, that an increase in product involvement will be accompanied by an increase in the proportion of inverted-U-shaped acceptability functions among both low- and high-income consumers.

The results of this study, based on about 280 consumers who responded to a paired-comparison task regarding 12 products, suggest highly consistent and reliable responses. For each product, a significantly higher proportion of higher-income consumers exhibit an inverted-U-shaped price acceptability function than low-income consumers. Further, the proportion of inverted-U-shaped functions varies significantly as a positive function of the level of involvement.

Ofir, Bechtel, and Winer (2000) adopt Thurstone's (1927) well-known method of successive intervals and Monroe's (1971a) classification method. Their basic assumption, in line with the pricing literature, is that consumers compare prices with latent thresholds. This assumption is explicit in Thurstone's method of successive intervals which, similar to Winer (1986), assumes heterogeneous price acceptability across consumers. Two functional relationships are obtained from the Ofir,

Bechtel, and Winer (2000) model: (1) the proportion of price acceptors at different price levels, and (2) the relation between subjective price acceptability and actual prices.

Some methods have been developed that focus exclusively on the upper threshold, that is, CV. The most direct approach is to ask a question such as, "What is the highest price you would be willing to pay for this product?" Some authors have studied potential judgmental biases with such an approach (e.g., Simonson and Drolet 2004). In particular, Posavac (2001) finds that the likelihood of overbidding of reservation prices was high when consumers perceived that they would not have to actually pay that price.

Other Approaches Economists have also estimated CV through what are called contingent valuation methods (e.g., Haneman 1994). These methods are applied most often to consumers' willingness to pay for pollution abatement, wildlife conservation, health care, and other public goods. Most of these studies use closed-ended questions such as "If it cost $5 million to clean up your neighborhood park, would you be willing to pay $100 per year in extra taxes to fund it?" Consumers (selected by random sampling) are offered different amounts, and the analysis of the results gives the distribution of willingness-to-pay.

Wertenbroch and Skiera (2002) develop a novel approach to estimating willingness-to-pay (or WTP) at point of purchase. They argue that in most procedures developed to elicit CV/WTP, there is no incentive for the respondent to give a truthful answer and that the simulated purchase situations are unrealistic. They develop what they term an "incentive-compatible" procedure in a realistic setting. In this procedure, customers are sampled at the point of purchase and are told that their buying price for a product, p, is not yet set and will be determined randomly. They are then asked to offer a price, s, for the product, which should be the most they are willing to pay for it. Then, p is determined through a random draw from a prespecified distribution of prices (unknown to the customers). If customers draw a p that is less than or equal to their offered price, s, they are required to buy it at p. If p exceeds their offer, s, they are not allowed to buy the product.

Thus, the customers have an incentive to give their true CV/WTP since (1) if the s offered is less than their true WTP, then their chances of buying at a gain are reduced (since more drawn p's will be greater than s), and (2) if the s offered is greater than the true WTP, then the chances of buying at a loss (drawn p greater than WTP but less than s) are increased. Spann, Skiera, and Schäfers (2004) extend this approach to name-your-own-price auction situations (e.g., Priceline).

The most common survey-based statistical approach to estimating price sensitivity is conjoint analysis (see, for example, Green and Srinivasan [1990]). In conjoint analysis, survey respondents are asked to either rank-order or provide some preference measure for a set of theoretical product profiles representing different combinations of product attributes. An example is shown in Figure 3. In this case, the respondent's evaluations (the far-right column) represented her preference orderings for the combinations of attributes of notebook computers. The respondent's sensitivity to the different price levels can be estimated by running a regression of the rank-order data against dummy variables

Figure 3
Conjoint Analysis: Notebook Computers

Assume three attributes of notebook computers:
Weight (2 pounds or 4 pounds)
Battery life (2 hours or 5 hours)
Brand name (IBM Thinkpad, Dell)

Task: Rank-order the following combinations of characteristics from 1 = most preferred to 8 = least preferred

Attribute Combinations	Preference Ordering
2 pounds, 2 hours, Thinkpad	4
4 pounds, 5 hours, Dell	5
4 pounds, 2 hours, Thinkpad	8
2 pounds, 5 hours, Thinkpad	3
2 pounds, 2 hours, Dell	2
4 pounds, 5 hours, Thinkpad	7
4 pounds, 2 hours, Dell	6
2 pounds, 5 hours, Dell	1

representing the different attribute levels. While standard conjoint analysis does not explicitly estimate a value for CV, by providing a reasonable spread on the price levels, a demand function by respondent, by segment, or across all respondents can be estimated.

Some variations of conjoint analysis have been developed to estimate CV (or something close to it) directly. For example, Jedidi and Zhang (2002) show how a conjoint analysis design like the one shown in Figure 3 could be adapted to produce estimates of reservation prices. Swait et al. (1993) estimate what they call "equalization prices," which express in monetary equivalents the utility difference attributed by the consumer to a brand relative to an undifferentiated, generic brand. This measure can be used to quantify the relative values consumers place on brands, that is, a relative CV.

Behavioral Response to Price

Many customers actively process price information; that is, they are not just price "takers" (to use the conventional microeconomic term). Customers continually assess the prices charged for products based on prior purchasing experience, formal communications (e.g., advertising) and informal communications (e.g., friends and neighbors), and point-of-purchase or Web-derived listings of prices; they use those assessments in their purchase decision.

Key concepts relating to the psychological aspects of pricing include price knowledge and judgments, "odd" pricing, reference price, fairness, price-quality perceptions, and context effects in price perceptions.

Price Knowledge and Judgments

Marketing researchers have attempted to assess the degree to which consumers remember prices of recently purchased products. A famous finding (Dickson and Sawyer 1990) is that a relatively low percentage of consumers can recall prices accurately even in the supermarket. This finding, which suggests that consumers do not pay attention to the prices they pay, disputes neoclassical economic thinking according to which consumers have complete knowledge of product prices (Marshall 1890).

Estelami, Lehmann, and Holden (2001) investigate the effects of macroeconomic and study design factors on consumer price knowledge. Using meta-analysis, they examine more than 200 studies and find that study design factors account for a significant reduction in percent average deviations from actual prices. These include monetary incentives and not allowing customers to respond to the price recall questions if they lack the necessary information to make a price judgment. A similar indication is suggested by Monroe (1976) regarding price comparison tasks among brands. Thus, simple task characteristics may have significantly biased Dickson and Sawyer's finding. Estelami, Lehmann, and

Holden also find that higher income levels are associated with lower levels of consumer price knowledge.

Vanhuele and Drèze (2002) also challenge the Dickson and Sawyer result by showing that price-recall studies focus on short-term memory, which significantly under-estimates price knowledge. By developing a method that accesses long-term price memory, the authors show that while customers may not recall exact prices, they possess a working knowledge of prices that is sufficiently accurate for good decisionmaking.

The competitive environment is shown to have an impact on how consumers form price judgments. Alba et al. (1994) investigate how consumers form judgments of how expensive a store is based on a market basket of goods and alternative pricing strategies: everyday low pricing (EDLP) versus Hi-Lo (regular retail prices using frequent temporary discounts). Although the two stores included in the study had equivalent market basket prices, consumers judged the prices in the Hi-Lo stores to be lower. In Alba et al. (1999), the authors add a longitudinal dimension to see how discounting patterns over time affect the results from the first study. In fact, the findings reverse: deep discounts (EDLP) lead to lower perceived prices than frequent, shallow discounts (Hi-Lo).

"Odd" Pricing

An interesting area of research focuses on how consumers process the digits of a price. A large number of studies documents that certain price endings (0, 5, 9) occur much more often than others. In particular, interest has centered around 9 endings, often called "odd" pricing. Odd pricing has been found to be an effective pricing strategy for retailers and in other settings as well. What explains the effectiveness of odd pricing in prompting consumer purchase? Two explanations—first, that consumers round prices down, essentially ignoring the right-hand digits, and second, that consumers discern meaning from prices that end in 9 (e.g., good value) and read prices from left to right—suggest that consumers use some heuristic to process the digits separately. Almost all other work in price assumes holistic processing.

Schindler and his co-authors (see, for example, Schindler and Kirby [1997]) use field experiments to infer why certain digits occur more often than others. Their findings suggest that the numbers 0 and 5 are used more frequently due to their high cognitive accessibility: round-number endings make price information easier for consumers to perceive, compare, and remember. Endings with 9 occur most frequently with prices with high potential underestimation, that is, where the 9s represent a large psychological drop in price from the price with one penny added (e.g., $49.99 versus $50.00). A more recent study by Anderson and Simester (2003) describes three field experiments manipulating catalogue prices. They found that the use of the $9 ending consistently increased demand across all three experiments, with the increase being the strongest for new items in the catalogue.

Thomas and Morwitz (2005) develop a conceptual framework based on the analog model of numerical cognition to explain why, say, $2.99 is perceived to be significantly cheaper than $3.00. The theory suggests that when two multi-digit numbers are compared, the quantitative meaning of the numbers is assessed by mapping them onto an internal analog magnitude scale. When this mapping occurs, left-to-right processing of the numbers distorts the price magnitude towards the leftmost digit.

A third approach to understanding odd pricing estimates empirical choice models with alternative formulations to capture different price processing heuristics (Stiving and Winer 1997). Using two frequently purchased product categories, the authors find consistent support for left-to-right price processing rather than holistic processing or rounding. These empirical results are consistent with the findings of Schindler and Kirby (1997) since a large psychological drop in price using a 9 would occur if left-to-right processing was being used.

Additionally, researchers have investigated the interpretation of promotions by consumers with implications for understanding odd pricing. Grewal, Marmorstein, and Sharma (1996) analyze the wording or semantic cues of discounts such as "was $50, now $34.99." They consider different contexts (e.g., in-home or in the store) and discount sizes. They find that semantic cues that make within-store price comparisons (as opposed to between-store comparisons) elicit a greater sense of value from consumers when consumers are situated in a retail store, but that between-store price comparisons are more effective when consumers are at home. Raghubir (1998) hypothesizes that consumers use the values of coupons to infer the retail prices of products. She finds that higher percentage discounts are associated with higher prices, which can undermine the effectiveness of the promotion.

Reference Prices

A reference price is any standard of comparison against which an observed price is judged. A number of psychological theories provide the conceptual underpinnings for this concept, including adaptation-level theory (Helson 1964) and assimilation-contrast theory (Sherif and Hovland 1953). Reference prices are internal (temporal) or external (contextual) (Rajendran and Tellis 1994; Briesch et al. 1997). External reference prices are usually the actual, observed prices; in a retailing setting, for example, these are typically posted at the point of purchase as the "regular retail price." Internal reference prices are mental prices used to assess an actual price. Some empirical work has found that different market segments use the internal and external reference prices differently (Mazumdar and Papatla 2000).

Reference price models generally use adaptation-level theory (Helson 1964) to assert that consumers compare observed prices to some internal reference point. However, Janiszewski and Lichtenstein (1999) propose that the range of price values can determine the value of any one price in the range. In other words, consumers may use a range of recalled price experiences to set a lower and upper bound of price expectations; in this case, the attractiveness of a particular observed price is a function of its location in the range. Winer (1988) proposes a number of internal reference prices. These include the "fair" price (what the product "ought" to cost the customer); the price frequently charged; the last price paid; the upper threshold, or highest amount a customer would pay (reservation price); the lower threshold, or lowest amount a customer would pay; the price of the brand usually bought; the average price charged for similar products; the expected future price; and the typical discounted price. Consumers may use one or more of these internal reference prices to construct the *perceived* price, a psychological concept that is the price the customer thinks is the current actual price of the product.

Consumer Choice Effects   While both internal and external reference prices have been found to significantly affect consumer choice (see, for example, Mayhew and Winer [1992] and Rajendran and Tellis [1994]), empirical research about which is more significant is mixed and seems to depend on the product category. In a comprehensive study, Briesch et al. (1997) estimate brand choice models using four different frequently purchased product categories and find that internal reference price provides a better fit than external reference price.

The research literature generally finds that reference price has a significant impact on brand choice of both durable and nondurable goods (see Kalyanaram and Winer [1995] for a review) and that it can have important normative implications (Greenleaf 1995). In particular, when the observed price is higher than the reference price, it can negatively affect purchasing because the consumer experiences this as an unpleasant surprise or perceives it to be a bad deal. For example, large price increases for cars in the 1970s created a sticker shock effect when consumer reference or perceived prices for cars were significantly lower than showroom prices. A happier situation occurs when the observed price is either at or below the reference price, as may happen when a brand a consumer intends to buy is promoted at a lower price.

The basic model used in reference price research is the following:

$$Prob_{ijt} = f \text{ (Brand dummy variables, brand loyalty,}$$
$$\text{marketing mix variables, } [RP_{ijt} - P_{ijt}], P_{ijt}),$$

where $Prob_{ijt}$ is the probability of household i purchasing brand j in week (or time period) t, P is the observed retail price, and RP is the reference or perceived price. The sticker shock effect occurs when P is higher than RP. The model also asserts that there is an impact of the observed price as well as the difference between RP and P.

Interestingly, following Kahneman and Tversky's prospect theory (1979), most empirical studies on reference price have found that unpleasant surprises have a greater impact on purchasing probabilities than pleasant surprises (see, for example, Mayhew and Winer [1992]). As can be seen from the prospect theory value function shown in Figure 4, losses are predicted to be valued more heavily than gains. Thus, the reference price model can be modified in the following way:

$$Prob_{ijt} = f \text{ (Brand dummy variables, brand loyalty,}$$
$$\text{marketing mix variables, } [RP_{ijt} - P_{ijt}]^+,$$
$$[RP_{ijt} - P_{ijt}]^-, P_{ijt}),$$

where the $[RP - P]$ term is split into two parts, one when the difference is positive and one when it is negative. According to prospect theory, the impact of the negatively signed difference should be greater than the impact of the difference with the positive sign.

Reference Price Asymmetry Krishnamurthy, Mazumdar, and Raj (1992) investigate segments in terms of the asymmetry of responses to reference price losses and gains. They find that brand loyals exhibit similar responses to losses and gains in brand choice but brand switchers respond more strongly to gains than losses. Mazumdar and Papatla (2000) find that consumers relying more on internal than external reference prices are more sensitive to gains than losses while those using external reference prices have the opposite behavior. In an extensive analysis across multiple product categories, Erdem, Mayhew, and Sun

Figure 4
Prospect Theory Function

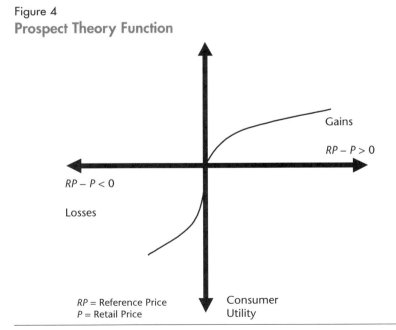

RP = Reference Price
P = Retail Price

(2001) find that loss-sensitive shoppers are less affected by past brand use and react more strongly to price, display, and newspaper feature advertising than the average consumer. Loss-sensitive shoppers tend to be from larger households with employed heads of household. Gain-sensitive households have similar responses to brand use, price, display, and feature advertising but to a lesser degree than the loss-sensitive households, and they have no clear demographic descriptors. Kopalle, Rao, and Assunção (1996) and Kopalle and Winer (1996) show the normative impact of reference price asymmetry. Two studies have questioned this result. Chang, Siddarth, and Weinberg (1999) and Bell and Lattin (2000) both find that heterogeneity in price responsiveness can potentially confound asymmetric reference price effects.

Expected Future Price A second important concept relating to reference price is expected future price. This is a particularly important concept for any product category that experiences significant price changes over time, for example, new consumer durables such as personal computers, camcorders, DVD players, etc. Customers are worried they will overpay, and discretionary purchasers can simply wait until the prices decrease as they are willing to forego the utility from owning the product sooner. This reference price concept has been studied much less in the literature, an exception being Winer (1985).

Fairness

One of the reference prices customers form is the fair price. When customers perceive a price to be unfair, their actions can have a significant negative impact on a firm. Those actions include not purchasing (thus significantly reducing lifetime customer value), spreading negative word-of-mouth, and engaging in other negative actions (Campbell 1999).

Research shows two main sources of perceived unfairness: (1) the vendor's perceived profit and (2) customers' inferences about the motives for the price (Campbell 1999). A sports team charging $5 for a small beer at a baseball game is an example of the former: the customer perceives that the vendor is making excess profits. Similarly, drug companies have been criticized for generating high profits from prescription drugs. A hardware store raising the price of an existing inventory of snow shovels during a snow storm is an example of the latter: consumers perceive that the store is price gouging or taking advantage of the misfortunes of its customers. Note that rational explanations for such increased prices, such as supply-demand conditions, are irrelevant since the concept of fairness is based on customer perception.

Bolton, Warlop, and Alba (2003) show in a series of experiments that consumers consistently believe that selling prices are higher than fair prices. This belief arises from consumers' knowledge of prices, costs, and estimates of profits in the marketplace. Interestingly, consumers systematically underestimate the impact of inflation on prices. Price differences are perceived to be the fairest if they can be attributed to differences in quality. Also, when consumers do consider costs, they consider only those costs associated with the cost of goods sold.

Xia, Monroe, and Cox (2004) developed a complete conceptual model of how customers form perceptions of price unfairness. This is shown in Figure 5. The process begins with a comparison to an external price (e.g., a competitor) or an internal standard (e.g., normal price paid). The output of this comparison is a judgment of the fairness of the price, both cognitive (i.e., thoughts, beliefs) and affective (emotional, e.g., anger). A number of variables potentially mediate the relationship between the comparison and the perceived price fairness judgment; these include the distribution of cost and profit and the historical relationship between the customer and the seller, among others. The perceived fairness judgment then creates an assessment of the perceived value of the seller's offering and possible negative emotions, and results in consumer action. When the judgment is negative and generates negative emotions, this action may include complaining or even legal action.

Price-Quality

Contrary to standard microeconomic theory, a higher price can sometimes lead to higher rather than lower demand, as when price is a quality signal. This often occurs under a condition of asymmetric information, that is, when the seller has more information about the true quality of the product or service than the buyer (Kirmani and Rao 2000). A strong perceived price-quality relationship may occur when a product's quality is difficult to assess before purchasing or difficult to assess at all. These products are often called experience goods (if you have to try the product before assessing its quality) or credence goods (if even after you have purchased and used the product or service, the quality is hard to evaluate). Examples of the former are most services, such as haircuts and legal advice. Examples of credence goods are car repairs such as brake servicing (the customer cannot actually see what happened) and wine (only experts can distinguish between different levels of quality). Marketers also use price to signal exclusivity or prestige. For example, Rolex could charge substantially less for its watches and still make a profit. However, Rolex prefers the prestige conferred by its prices (thousands of dollars for a watch) and the resulting "exclusivity" of owners.

There is a long tradition of academic research on the price-quality relationship (see Leavitt 1954). Integrative reviews (e.g., Rao and

Figure 5
Price Fairness: A Conceptual Framework

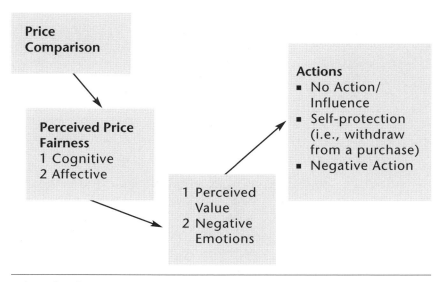

Adapted with permission from the *Journal of Marketing*, published by the American Marketing Association. Lan Xia, Kent B. Monroe, and Jennifer L. Cox (2004), "The Price Is Unfair! A Conceptual Framework of Price Fairness Perceptions," *Journal of Marketing* 68 (October), 1–15.

Monroe 1989) have generally found that there is a statistically significant relationship between price and perceived quality. More recent work has focused on mediating factors that might attenuate the relationship. For example, Kardes et al. (2004) show in an experimental context that the relationship between price and perceived quality is reduced the greater the quantity of information presented to respondents, if that information is presented in a random order, and when concern for closure is low (when respondents could take as much time as needed to make their judgments).

Purchasing Context Effects

Research finds that customer decisionmaking can vary greatly in different purchasing contexts. For example, in an experiment simulating purchasing decisions, whether or not respondents decide to purchase an expensive watch will depend on how much income they are given in the simulation. The reason for the purchase also defines the context: people's behavior when purchasing a product for themselves is different from their behavior when the purchase is a gift. Huber, Payne, and Puto (1982) show that the introduction of a new product can change the shopping context and affect the sales of incumbent products in interesting ways. In an example from their study:

> A store owner has two camel hair jackets priced at $100 and $150 and finds that the more expensive jacket is not selling. A new camel hair jacket is added and displayed for $250; the new jacket does not sell, but sales of the $150 jacket increase (p. 95).

The new choice context produces the surprising result that an incumbent product's value to customers is enhanced by introducing a more expensive option.

Figure 6 shows how willingness-to-pay can be affected by the purchasing context (Gourville 1999). The only difference in the scenarios depicted is the location where the beer is purchased: a small, run-down grocery store or a fancy resort hotel. The median response in the grocery store context is $1.50; in the fancy hotel it is $2.65.

Figure 6
Two Psychological Pricing Scenarios

Scenario #1:
You are lying on the beach on a hot day. All you have to drink is ice water. For the past hour, you have been thinking about how much you would enjoy a nice cold bottle of your favorite beer. A friend gets up to make a phone call and offers to bring back a bottle of your favorite beer from the only nearby place where beer is sold—**a small, rundown grocery store**. He says that the beer might be expensive and asks how much you are willing to spend. He says he will not buy the beer if it costs more than the price you state. What price do you tell your friend?

Scenario #2:
You are lying on the beach on a hot day. All you have to drink is ice water. For the past hour, you have been thinking about how much you would enjoy a nice cold bottle of your favorite beer. A friend gets up to make a phone call and offers to bring back a bottle of your favorite beer from the only nearby place where beer is sold—**a fancy resort hotel**. He says that the beer might be expensive and asks how much you are willing to spend. He says he will not buy the beer if it costs more than the price you state. What price do you tell your friend?

Adapted and reprinted by permission: Richard H. Thaler (1985), "Mental Accounting and Consumer Choice," *Marketing Science* 4 (Summer), 199–214. © 1985, the Institute for Operations Research and the Management Sciences, 7240 Parkway Drive, Suite 310, Hanover, Maryland 21076.

Pricing Tactics

Managers use a variety of modifications of "normal" list price. These include bundling and unbundling, flat-rate versus per-use charges, price-matching guarantees and refunds, strategies based on customer currency valuation, and yield management strategies.

Bundling

In price bundling, a package of goods and services (e.g., a McDonald's no. 1 meal) is charged a price that is lower than the combined prices of those goods or services priced separately. Bundling has been studied extensively by marketing academics. Stremersch and Tellis (2002, p. 56) define bundling as:

> the sale of two or more separate products in one package. Separate products are defined as products for which separate markets exist.

In addition, the notion of bundling used here, a special price for a package of goods and/or services, can be distinguished from product bundling ,which is the integration and sale of two or more distinct products or services at any price. Stremersch and Tellis (2002) argue that price bundling is an optimal strategy since it price-discriminates between different segments that have different reservation prices for the components of the bundle. Thus, the seller can extract a surplus from a customer who pays a price higher than his or her WTP for one or more individual items to get other items in the bundle.

For example, assume two products, 1 and 2, and two customers, A and B. A has a WTP for product 1 of $20 but only $10 for product 2. B values both 1 and 2 in the middle, say, at $15. If both products are sold for $15, B buys both and A buys only product 1, so the company generates $45 in revenues. If the company bundles products 1 and 2 together for $29, the bundle is below the reservation prices of both customers A and B, and the company will generate $58 in revenues.

Bundling may also increase purchase likelihood for any one item since the utility for the bundle may be greater than the sum of the individual product utilities. For example, a home entertainment system may contain a DVD player that the customer would not otherwise purchase. With an HDTV, surround sound, amplifier, etc., the bundle is attractive, and the DVD is purchased as part of the system.

Stremersch and Tellis (2002) also find that price bundling produces greater profit increases the higher the contribution margins and economies of scale and scope. Therefore, services or products with high development costs but low marginal costs, such as software, gain more from price bundling than products with higher marginal costs, such as consumer durables or industrial goods. Bakos and Brynjolfsson (1999) report a similar finding for bundling information goods.

In some cases, a bundled price offer discounts one item of a pair of complementary items, for example, a razor/blades bundle in which the razor is offered at full price and the blades at a discount. Research shows that it matters which item is full price and which is discounted (Janiszewski and Cunha 2004). Assuming that the customer differentially weights the products in the bundle (Yadav 1994), the impact of a price discount on the overall bundle evaluation will be greater when the discount is given for the more important product.

An interesting question arises when a price bundle is created for a service such as a sports or theater series subscription: How much of the series is actually consumed (attended)? Soman and Gourville (2001) show that customers are more likely to forego consumption (and demand less compensation) for an individual benefit that is bought in a bundle. They study the behavior of skiers who make a multiple-day lift ticket purchase at a ski resort. One customer buys a four-day pass and the other buys four one-day lift tickets for the same total cost. Both customers ski for three days, and on the fourth day the weather is poor. Which customer is more likely to ski? The total prepaid cost is the same. Soman and Gourville show that the skier who paid for the one-day lift tickets is more likely to ski, because he or she can attach a value to the fourth day with less ambiguity than the one who bought the pass. They refer to the disassociation of costs and benefits in a price-bundling context as "transaction decoupling."

Unbundling

In unbundling, a company charges separate prices for individual parts of a product. For example, online music services such as iTunes and Rhapsody let customers purchase individual songs rather than a complete CD. In another example, a refrigerator, icemaker, and warranty can be priced separately. While the economic arguments above favor a bundled price, some results from psychology show that unbundled prices can result in higher overall product evaluations and greater choice (Chakravarti et al. 2002).

Unbundling can also be used to make a large expense look small by advertising or framing it in terms of the smaller amounts. For example, a $1,000 fitness club membership may be promoted as costing only $3 each day. Gourville (1998) calls this the "pennies-a-day," or PAD strategy. Future research might examine reverse PAD strategies for undesirable products (e.g., showing how much cigarette users spend annually versus a per-pack mentality).

Partitioned prices are another unbundling strategy; with price partitioning, one price is charged for a product and another for shipping and handling. Interestingly, Morwitz, Greenleaf, and Johnson (1998) show that partitioned prices decrease customers' recalled total costs and increase their demand. Services can also be partitioned, as when an access price is separated from a usage price. Utilizing data from a field experiment, Danaher (2002) finds that for a cellular phone service, access price has a much stronger impact on retention (and the customer churn rate) than the usage price, while the usage price primarily affects monthly usage quantity, as expected.

Flat-Rate and Per-Use Pricing

An interesting pricing dilemma, particularly for subscription services, is whether to charge a flat fee or on a per-use basis. For example, some cellular phone service providers offer prepaid plans in which customers pay a flat fee for a fixed number of minutes per month. AOL has moved from an access fee-usage plan to a monthly flat rate with unlimited usage.

Flat-rate plans may be attractive to customers for a number of reasons, including the desire to reduce transaction costs (convenience) and not worry about how much they are using a service, thus increasing their enjoyment. Risk-averse customers may hedge against an abnormally high bill by paying a flat rate.

However, numerous empirical studies show a "flat-rate bias" (Train 1991): customers systematically overestimate their usage of such subscription services, incorrectly choosing a flat rate over a per-use rate. In one study, while most flat-rate customers generate significantly more monthly usage, approximately 10–15% are incorrectly choosing that plan (Kridel, Lehman, and Weisman 1993). In another study (Train 1991), 65% of customers choosing a flat-rate pricing plan would have been better off using some kind of measured service.

In a series of studies, Nunes (2000) shows that two cognitive errors interfere with respondents' accurately predicting their future usage. First, rather than comparing their average rate or long-term expectation of usage with the break-even usage level, they compare the subjective probability of using more than the break-even number with the subjective probability of using less. Second, they overestimate the incidence in the population of higher-than-average usage. The actual distributions of customers' usage rates is likely to be the opposite of their expectations. This is particularly true of new and inexperienced users.

Meyvis and Xie (2005) examine how customers switch between the two kinds of pricing plans over time. They show that in experimental conditions in which two plans are equally financially attractive, customers find it easier to switch from a measured (linear) usage rate to a flat rate than the reverse. One possible explanation is that people may feel worse about reducing their usage of a service if they switch to a metered pricing scheme than they do about paying more money for a flat rate. This is consistent with the literature on price promotions that shows that customers are less willing to sacrifice quality for price than to sacrifice price for quality.

Lambrecht and Skiera's (2005) findings support those of earlier studies showing the flat-rate bias; the researchers examine the impact of customer churn, that is, customers dropping their current service provider, on this rate bias. Their empirical results on churn are asymmetric. Using a number of different sets of data, they show that customers mistakenly paying the higher flat rate do not significantly increase their churn rate, resulting in both a short- and long-term increase in company profits. In contrast, customers who mistakenly choose the pay-per-use rate have a greater churn rate, thus providing greater short-term profits but lower profits in the long term.

Price-Matching Guarantees and Refunds

Retailers often offer to match a lower price customers bring from a competitor, or offer a refund for the price difference. Such retailer-originated programs are normally widely communicated as part of store policy. These price-matching guarantees or refunds may also exist in industrial markets when there is competitor-matching language in sales contracts.

A number of explanations are offered for the use of price-matching refunds or guarantees (Jain and Srivastava 2000). Two are driven by economic theory, which predicts that prices will be higher when such price-matching policies exist. First, in an oligopolistic competitive scenario, price-matching policies reduce firms' incentives to lower retail prices; therefore price-matching policies maximize joint profits. This collusive practice helps the retailers to maintain high prices. A second explanation, based upon price discrimination, assumes two groups of customers—one group that has high search costs and is price insensitive and another that has low search costs and is highly price elastic. The price-matching policy allows the retailer to charge the optimal price to both groups. This is because the price-insensitive group will not spend the time trying to find a lower price and will pay the posted price while the price-sensitive group will perform some comparative price search.

In contrast, retailers widely believe that price-matching policies actually instigate price competition and can lead to lower prices. This has been shown theoretically (e.g., Hviid and Shaffer 1999; Chen, Narasimhan, and Zhang 2001) and in practice, i.e., the introduction of these policies has sometimes led to price wars.

Jain and Srivastava (2000) use experimental evidence to rationalize these diverging viewpoints. They show that consumers perceive store prices to be lower, have higher store purchase intentions, and perceive greater store choice in the presence of price-matching guarantees. In addition, Jain and Srivastava develop a model that shows that in a competitive market, only those stores with the lowest prices have an incentive to offer such guarantees. Srivastava and Lurie (2001) present experimental evidence showing that such guarantees also increase store search when search costs are low.

Customer Currency Valuation Effects

People spend more money when a monetary value is broken up into small amounts than when it is represented by a large denomination. Raghubir and Srivastava (2004) call this the denomination effect. They show in one experiment that 71% of subjects would spend four quarters on candy but only 29% would spend the same amount in the form of a dollar bill.

Albert and Winer (2005) describe a new technology, based on this notion, that encourages customers to spend their spare change at the point of purchase. Fast-food restaurants, including Burger King, KFC, Taco Bell, Wendy's, and others, use software that makes real-time sales pitches based on the change the customer is about to receive. For example, if a customer orders a meal for $4.29, the software, which runs on a cash register, instantly generates a discount offer for another food item based on the change (71 cents) that would be returned on an even amount ($5 in this case). If, for example, French fries normally cost a dollar, the system might offer to add fries to the order for 71 cents and round the total order up to an even $5.

The offer is developed from a continually updated database of previous offers and acceptance rates. If the system discovers that more customers who have bought a hamburger will buy French fries with the resulting spare change than will buy a milk shake, for instance, it will preferentially offer French fries to future hamburger buyers. A proprietary study finds that stores using this technology increase sales by 3–5%, and pretax profits by 30%. Approximately 35% of all spare-change offers are accepted and most of the time customers pay 35–45% less for the added item than if they had bought it separately.

Other research has explored a variety of topics in the area of how consumers value currencies. Raghubir and Srivastava (2002) explore how people spend different foreign currencies relative to their home currency. There is no general tendency to under- or overspend; however, they find in a number of experiments that subjects overspend when the currency is a fraction of their home currency (say, four units to the dollar) and underspend when the currency is a multiple of their currency (say, one unit equals two dollars). Prelec and Simester (2001) demonstrate that WTP can be increased when subjects must pay by credit card rather than with cash, particularly in situations where the product or service in question has an uncertain market value. Drèze and Nunes (2004) examine conditions under which companies can maximize revenues using combined currencies. For example, an airline might sell a flight for a combination of money and frequent flier miles.

Yield Management

Services are perishable. When a service is not performed at a particular time, the revenue is lost forever and cannot be recaptured. For example, when a seat at a baseball game is unfilled, that revenue is foregone. Services also usually have capacity constraints. Hotels have a fixed number of rooms; a baseball stadium has a fixed number of seats, etc.

These two characteristics of services have led to the development of a pricing strategy called yield management. Yield management uses sophisticated pricing algorithms and information technology to determine the optimal prices to charge and capacity to offer at different points in time. For example, a hotel with empty rooms on a particular day in the future must decide what price to charge over a time horizon prior to that day. Managers have to balance perishability (you need to fill all the seats), which puts downward pressure on price, with capacity constraint (you have a limited number of seats), which permits you to charge a higher price for a popular service. In these circumstances, yield management strategies often give lower prices for early purchases and raise the prices as the date of use approaches.

In an analysis of yield management systems, Desiraju and Shugan (1999) define two market segments, the price-insensitive (PI) segment and the price-sensitive (PS) segment. They also define three service classes A, B, and C. Class A is characterized by early purchases by the PS segment. Airlines and hotels would fall into this group. Class B is characterized by early purchases by the PI segment. Services for which a high value is attached to purchasing just after introduction, such as cellular phone service and fashion retailing, would be Class B. Class C services purchases do not correlate with either PS or PI. These would include repair services (you have to have them when you need them).

Three major findings of their analysis are:

1. For Class A services, the best pricing policy is to charge an initially low price but restrict capacity that can be sold at that price. These prices should then increase over time. This is a profit-maximizing strategy when the PI segment is large but less than full capacity. Of the three classes of services, Class A services are most ideally suited to yield management practices.

2. For Class B services, the pricing policy starts out high for the PI segment and is lowered over time to draw in the PS segment. This is similar to the pricing strategy followed by high-end retailers who take markdowns until inventory is sold out. Yield management does not maximize profits.

3. For Class C services (such as repair services), purchasers arrive randomly as their need dictates, so there is no pattern for either PS or PI customers. Optimal pricing is based upon the WTP of the average customer, adjusted as necessary due to competition, costs, etc. Again, yield management policies are not suitable.

Koenigsberg, Muller, and Vilcassim (2004) examine yield management policies in the context of easyJet, a popular, low-cost short-haul airline in Europe. easyJet's pricing policy is simple: fares are quoted one-way only and the price that is given for a seat at any point in time has no restrictions. However, the prices are controlled by yield management policies, and increase the closer to the date of the flight. This pattern is shown in Figure 7.

Figure 7
Illustration of Yield Management

Sales (# of seats and price) for one-way airline ticket, Liverpool, U.K. to Alicante, Spain, departing January 27, 2003

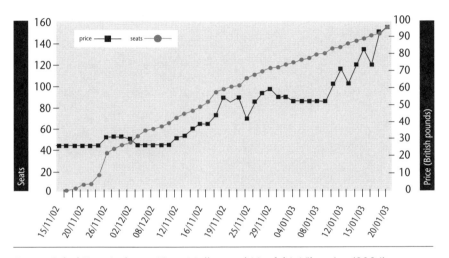

From: Oded Koenigsberg, Eitan Muller, and Naufel J. Vilcassim (2004), "easyJet Airlines: Small, Lean, and with Prices That Increase over Time," New York, N.Y.: Columbia University, Working Paper.

Using a dynamic pricing model, the authors show that the price increase should be a direct function of the number of seats left on the flight, and that having last-minute specials is not optimal.

Empirical Research on Price

As long as marketing academics have estimated market response functions, price response—in the form of elasticities or other measures—has been a topic of interest. The widely cited Guadagni and Little (1983) paper sparked new interest in price response because of its focus on brand choice.[4] A meta-analysis of 10 years' research (Tellis 1988) shows that average price elasticity is about eight times larger (in absolute value) than advertising elasticity (see also Assmus, Farley, and Lehmann [1984]).

Empirical research on price at the brand or store level has continued at a brisk pace; recent topics include the interaction of advertising and price, retailing issues, price search by consumers, and methodological advances.

Interaction of Advertising and Price

Two competing hypotheses describe the interaction between advertising and price. The first, termed the market power hypothesis, is that advertising creates brand loyalty and product differentiation and, therefore, lowers price elasticities. The second is that advertising is information and as such increases consideration sets and competition, thereby creating greater price sensitivity. A considerable amount of empirical research on both theories has produced mixed results (Kaul and Wittink 1995). For example, Mela, Gupta, and Lehmann (1997) find that advertising decreases price sensitivity in their data. Kalra and Goodstein (1998) examine different advertising positioning strategies and find that only a value-oriented positioning decreases willingness-to-pay.

These results may be rationalized by examining the kind of advertising used. Price-oriented advertising, not unexpectedly, leads to greater price sensitivity, while advertising that is not price oriented has the reverse effect. Consumer behavior may also come into play: Mitra and Lynch (1995) reconcile the different results by hypothesizing two mediating effects: the size of the consideration set and the strength of underlying brand preferences.

Conventional wisdom holds that sales promotion, being price focused, should have a negative interaction with advertising. Assuming a choice model context, Naik, Raman, and Winer (2005) model the advertising-promotion interaction as follows:

$$Prob_{ijt} = f \text{ (brand dummy variables, brand loyalty,}$$
$$Adv_{ijt}, Promo_{ijt}, Adv_{ijt} \times Promo_{ijt}, \text{ other}$$
$$\text{marketing variables).}$$

In this model, there are separate main effects: those of advertising and promotion on brand choice probabilities, both presumably positive, and the interaction effects of advertising and promotion, which should be negative.[5]

In a dynamic, competitive framework, the authors find empirical support for this notion and show that it has significant implications for optimal spending. In particular, for one product category, they find that when interaction effects are accounted for, large brands underadvertise and overspend on promotion, while small brands both underadvertise and underpromote.

Retailing Issues

The increased availability of electronic scanner data and interest in micromarketing (product assortments customized to the local clientele) have generated research focusing on the retailer's pricing problem. Hoch et al. (1995) estimate store-level price elasticities for 18 product categories from a chain of 83 supermarkets. They find that 11 demographic and competitive variables explain two-thirds of the variation in elasticities, thus providing empirical support for the micromarketing concept. Montgomery (1997) improves the estimation procedure for store price elasticities with hierarchical Bayes estimation and, using a normative model, shows that micromarketing strategies can increase gross profits anywhere from 3.9–10% over a uniform chain pricing strategy.

Other retailing issues relate to types of store promotions, such as off-the-shelf price discounts automatically deducted at the checkout and in-store coupons available near the product. In a series of field experiments, Dhar and Hoch (1996) show that on average, coupons increase sales by 35% and retailer profits by 108%. Little other work of this type has been done.

Chintagunta (2002) incorporates three factors affecting retailer pricing behavior for one supermarket chain: (1) the effects of payments from manufacturers to the retailer, (2) the retailer's objectives for its private-label brand, and (3) the effects of retail competition. Using data on weekly chain traffic, unit sales, retail prices, and manufacturer prices to the retailer, he finds that the effects of these factors vary across brands in the product category studied.

Pricing Decision Support Systems

Real-time information on sales by stockkeeping unit (SKU) by store has provided the basis for pricing decision support systems (PDSSs) that make possible rapid pricing updates. In this type of market response model brand sales are modeled as a function of various factors—promotion, in-store displays, advertising spending, day of the week, as well as price and other factors that can affect the brand's sales. With continuously updated sales and price data (plus information on the other control variables), the response function is employed to determine the optimal price at a given point in time.

Montgomery (2004) lists a number of qualifications for a good PDSS. In the pricing context, users of a PDSS must be able to interact with the system and simulate the impact of different pricing policy scenarios. Users must also be able to see how changes in price for an individual brand in a line affects the whole line and to adjust line prices accordingly; the PDSS must enable them to coordinate across complementary product categories and stores, and it must be able to recommend optimal pricing strategies.

There are, naturally, a number of challenges to the adoption of PDSSs. The amount of data collected across SKUs, stores, and over time presents an enormous data management challenge, even in 2005. Additionally, since the parameters of the models are estimated using historical data, they are subject to the usual caveats about such forecasts. Changing prices at the retail level is not a trivial task. Price tags still need to be placed at the point of purchase. While exciting developments in digital paper are occurring that would permit price changes to be transmitted directly to signage, such technology is not in widespread use yet. This is only a subset of the issues that need to be resolved. However, an increased number of retailers are using PDSSs.

Price Search

An interesting area of pricing research at the consumer level is price search. Prior work in this area has relied on Stigler's search theory (1961): people will search for price information to the point where the marginal benefits from search equal the marginal costs. Urbany, Dickson, and Kalapurakal (1996) propose a model of price search incorporating three broad sets of factors: habit, noneconomic returns to search (e.g., shopping enjoyment), and economic returns. They find that the first two help to explain price search behavior better than in previous studies which had relied only on economic returns. Bronnenberg and Vanhonacker (1996) incorporate search into a two-stage logit model of brand choice, where the first stage is the consideration set (that is, for how many brands the household actually searches for price) and the second stage is brand choice. They find that response to variations in shelf price is limited to the brands in the choice or consideration set. (For a discussion of price search behavior on the Internet, see "Pricing and the Internet.")

Methodological Advances

A considerable amount of effort in the pricing area has been devoted to improving methods for estimating price elasticities. Kalyanam and Shively (1998) take a stochastic spline approach to better estimate price response functions that are often far from smooth due to promotions, small price variations around category price points, etc. Montgomery and Rossi (1999) use Bayesian methods to improve the estimation of store-based price elasticities.

Some work has incorporated dynamic programming into choice models. For example, Erdem, Imai, and Keane (2003) assume that consumers form price expectations and solve for optimal purchase timing, brand choice, and purchase quantity decisions. Applying their model to a frequently purchased product category, the authors find that estimates of price and cross-price elasticities are sensitive to how households form expectations of future prices and to the underlying stochastic process for actual prices.

Game-Theoretic Models

As competition in most markets has intensified, much has been written about how to deal with competitor moves in pricing. For example, Rao, Bergen, and Davis (2000) discuss price wars in markets such as cellular phone service. As a result, there has been increased interest in the past decade in applying game-theoretic methods, which incorporate competition, to pricing issues. Game theory allows researchers to characterize equilibria under various assumptions about competitive actions and reactions in a way that is not possible using more static, empirically based, models. The disadvantage of incorporating competitive interactions is that institutional richness may be sacrificed for model solvability. In this regard, however, the NEIO (New Economic Industrial Organization) models (see, for example, Sudhir [2001]) combine game theory and empirical analysis to estimate of the impact of competitive interactions.

Most game-theoretic papers, not surprisingly, include some aspect of pricing in them, and pricing is a particularly strong component in two areas of this research—channels of distribution and product policy issues. While some of this work has an empirical component, what separates it from the research described in the previous section is that the theoretical model is based on the competitive interactions described above.

Channels of Distribution

Game-theoretic modeling is commonly used to examine the role of price as a coordination mechanism in the manufacturer- retailer channel. Lee and Staelin (1997) develop a model with two manufacturers selling competing products to two competing retailers. More recently, Raju and Zhang (2005) examine the situation that a manufacturer faces when there is a powerful retailer like a Wal-Mart in the channel system.

Game theory is also applied to modeling how supermarkets compete using either an EDLP (everyday low pricing) format or a Hi-Lo (regular prices with in-store promotions) format. Lal and Rao (1997) examine the conditions under which EDLP can be successful, assuming two segments of consumers: time-constrained consumers and "cherry pickers" who seek the lowest prices. They show that EDLP stores use lower basket prices to attract both segments, while Hi-Lo stores use service to compete in the time-constrained segment and price specials to compete in the cherry-picking segment.

For a firm having a channel system other than direct sales, channel power may be held by either the firm or the channel. In this regard, there has been considerable interest among marketers in the "New Empirical Industrial Organization" literature in economics that specifies a model with strategic interactions common to game theory. Kadiyali, Chintagunta, and Vilcassim (2000) develop a method of measuring channel member power and of explaining the underlying reasons for that power. They find that for two grocery items, the retailer's market power is very significant.

Bargaining among channel members, as when retailers try to extract better promotional allowances or manufacturers try to get more shelf space, is another area for modeling. Srivastava, Chakravarti, and Rapoport (2000) adapt a game-theoretic model (sequential equilibrium) to predict bargaining behavior and outcomes for a scenario in which a manufacturer and an exclusive, independent distributor are negotiating the transfer or wholesale price of a new product. In experiments, however, they find that players bargained suboptimally, took longer to agree, and differed in a number of other respects. This experimental economics approach to understanding bargaining situations is a fruitful avenue for future research.

Desai and Purohit (2004) examine a situation in which two competing automobile dealers offer fixed prices or permit haggling, that is, negotiated prices. Their model has two segments, which permits sellers to discriminate on price. The two segments are hagglers, who like to bargain due to their low opportunity cost of time and other lower haggling costs, and nonhagglers. Even though haggling results in higher costs for the dealer (i.e., salesperson and manager time), the authors show that if the proportion of nonhagglers is sufficiently high, it pays to offer the haggling option to those who want it. (This may explain why the option of negotiating prices exists widely in the automobile industry in spite of the fact that a J. D. Power study shows that 68% of auto buyers do not like to negotiate.)

Product Policy Issues

Academics have also used game theory to study a variety of pricing issues relating to product policy, each of which opens up a potential area for research. Vandenbosch and Weinberg (1995) extend prior game theory work looking at product differentiation as a single dimension that tends toward maximization. Using two dimensions, product positioning and price, they find that firms should choose maximum differentiation on one of the two dimensions and minimum differentiation on the other. An interesting product policy question is how to price products that have branded components such as "Intel inside" Compaq personal computers (Venkatesh and Mahajan 1997). Desiraju and Shugan (1999) examine the pricing problems facing service companies such as airlines, which lose revenue forever when a plane takes off with empty seats (also see the subsection on yield management in the earlier chapter on pricing tactics). Krishnan, Bass, and Jain (1999) take the Generalized Bass Model (Bass, Krishnan, and Jain 1994) and develop optimal pricing policies for new product introductions.

Pricing and the Internet

U.S. retail sales on the Internet in the first quarter of 2005 were nearly $20 billion, 2.2% of all retail sales (U.S. Census Bureau 2005).[6] The increased penetration of broadband technology and the Web has created a new pricing environment for marketing managers.[7] The notion of a fixed price for all customers has virtually disappeared in favor of personalized pricing. In this price-competitive world, shopping agents can check for the lowest price, and customers can specify the prices they are willing to pay. Further, lower search costs create an environment in which it is very easy to comparison-shop—even without shopping agents.

In many product categories, consumers are able to save significant amounts of money with more convenience. In two studies, Scott Morton, Zettelmeyer, and Silva-Russo (2001, 2005) report that automobile buyers using online services saved on average 1.5–2% relative to those purchasing cars offline using no information from the Web. In some product areas such as news, sports, and other content, competitors are charging a price of zero. Bakos (2001) describes the major implications of the Internet for pricing as follows:

To begin, buyer search costs are reduced since it is easy and efficient to move from one Web e-commerce site to another, from one retail store to another. Some websites, such as Shopping.com (electronics) and Expedia (travel), make search particularly efficient in their product categories. Lower search costs enable customers to consider more product options and better match their needs to products. With lower search costs, price competition on the Web is intensified, particularly for products and services that are difficult to differentiate. This is clearly a benefit to customers.

To escape intense price competition, there is increased pressure to differentiate on the basis of information, product selection, customer service, brand name, and other nonprice dimensions. For example, Amazon.com, although it does not offer the lowest prices for books or CDs, has added value through brand building and shopping convenience (as in its one-click purchasing process). In this regard, Alba et al. (1997) suggest five possible approaches to seeking competitive advantage in electronic retailing: distribution efficiency, assortments of complementary merchandise, collection and utilization of customer information, presentation of information through electronic formats, and unique merchandise.

Dynamic Pricing

A reduction in search costs increases the firm's ability to target customers more accurately (Chen and Sudhir 2004). The Web offers enormous potential for price discrimination. When a customer registers for a site, generating an information cookie on his or her computer, the online seller can customize information (e.g., promotional offers), products, and prices to that customer. Some sites offer different prices to different shoppers at the same site for the same product depending upon the shoppers' past history, the prices of the products being examined, and the sites from which they came. For example, if a customer visits a site and does a price comparison, the site may automatically adjust its prices to the lowest price as it senses that the customer is price elastic.

This type of dynamic pricing, while it has the potential to optimize profits, raises interesting issues regarding brand equity and the ethical dimensions of price discrimination. Although it is not illegal to price-discriminate to end-customers, it may weaken brand equity, as in 2000, when Amazon customers discovered they were receiving different prices. The consumer outcry forced Amazon to disclose its behavior although the company did not indicate that it would refrain from such activity in the future. It is also illegal to tie the pricing mechanism to demographics such as race, resulting in a kind of electronic redlining. Interestingly, the Web can, in some cases, level the playing field: Scott Morton and Zettelmeyer (2003) show that African-American and Hispanic customers pay more than other offline customers for automobiles but that this difference disappears online.

An interesting perspective on how much to invest in price customization is offered by Chen and Iyer (2002). Using a game-theoretic model with two competitors, they argue that firms will not want to invest too little or too much in customer addressability (ability to target individual customers) to offer customized prices. Clearly, if they invest too little they miss price discrimination opportunities. The insight is that if the competitors invest too much to identify the best customers in the market, it will create ruinous price competition since both firms (assuming a duopoly) will be pursuing the same customers.

Pricing Mechanisms

Dolan and Moon (2000) conceptualize Internet pricing structures; the discussion below is based largely on their framework.

The Set Price Mechanism   For any individual customer, most retail websites, such as the Barnes & Noble site (bn.com), offer fixed prices for their products, and the customer can choose to buy or not buy at the posted prices (note that these fixed prices can vary over customers, as noted in our discussion above). These sites are heavily affected by price search tools such as MySimon.com, as it is simple for the customer to find the lowest price available for the product. Except for the customer segment that is uninformed about these price-comparison mechanisms, such retail websites must either match the lowest price available or add value through branding or some other approach, as described above.

Buyer-Seller Negotiations   Online price negotiation offers an alternative to face-to-face interactions, which many people dislike. During the Internet boom period, sites such as NexTag offered real-time price negotiations. A shopper could view prices different vendors were offering for a particular product, counter with a lower price, and give vendors an opportunity to bid on the transaction. Although NexTag is now a standard price-comparison site and other sites offering such real-time price negotiations have disappeared, this remains an interesting online pricing option.

Exchanges   In exchanges, a group of buyers and sellers interact in electronic marketplaces to trade and set prices for transactions. Most of the Internet sites in this category are designed around a particular industry such as metals, steel, and automobile parts. Companies such as Ariba and Commerce One have been very successful in this segment providing software tools for companies to manage their supply chains.

Micropayments   The Internet has made it simpler to charge small amounts of money (micropayments) for unbundled products or information, including bits of online content such as individual songs or stories from newspapers. The payment system PayPal was designed to handle such payments easily and has been reasonably successful; it was purchased by eBay in 2002 and has 72 million worldwide accounts, compared with American Express's 65 million (Hof 2005). Other companies such as BitPass and Peppercoin offer similar services.

Micropayments are attractive to both sellers and buyers because (1) the customer pays only for what he or she wants and (2), assuming Gourville's pennies-a-day theory, a micropayment looks more attractive than a larger purchase (such as the entire CD or content subscription). However, there are additional transaction costs for buyers, such as the cost of registering for PayPal and of maintaining the account (see also Szabo [1999]). More research is needed on this topic.

Internet Auctions   Online auctions are one of the most popular innovations of the Internet. eBay, the leader in online auctions, generates more than $20 billion in sales annually and has a market capitalization at the time of this writing of $47 billion. In online auctions, competition among buyers and sellers results in prices that vary widely across transactions. Online auctions take one of two forms. In the classic English auction model, competition among buyers leads to a price. The classic auction has been around for hundreds, if not thousands, of years. In a reverse auction, sellers compete for a buyer's business. A noteworthy example is Priceline.com, which started with auctions for airline seats and has moved to hotel rooms, rental cars, and cruises.

The topic of auctions has been an active area of research for economists since Vickrey's 1961 paper describing basic auction mechanisms. More-recent papers in the marketing and economics literatures shed light on research areas related to Internet auctions. One stream of literature relates to the basic auction format (Lucking-Reiley 1999). In addition to the English and reverse auctions, other auction mechanisms include Dutch, first-price sealed-bid, and second-price sealed-bid. In a Dutch auction, which is conducted in real time, a public price clock starts at a very high level and falls until a participant bids. In sealed-bid auctions, bidders submit bids by a deadline. In the first-price auction, the highest bidder wins. In the second-price auction, the winning bidder pays the second-highest bid. Vickrey (1961) shows that under some standard bidding assumptions, the expected auctioneer revenue is the same in all four formats. However, using a real Internet context (magic game cards), Lucking-Reiley (1999) shows that the Dutch auction format produces significantly higher revenues than the others, violating the theoretical predictions.

In a series of papers, Bajari and Hortaçu (2003, 2004) report general findings from economic analyses of Internet auctions. First, informational asymmetries—in which one party has more information than the other—are important in online auctions. In an English auction such as those on eBay, the seller has more information on the quality of the product being auctioned than the buyer. (On eBay, this potential problem is mitigated by sellers' ratings and other information exchange that drive out—for the most part—bad sellers.) Because of this, ratings of sellers is important information to prospective buyers (Bruce, Haruvy, and Rao 2004). Second, due to informational asymmetries, there is a significant possibility for "winner's curse"—when bidders overestimate the true value of the good being sold, and the highest bidder overpays for the item. This is most likely to occur for an item that attracts naïve bidders. Third, ascending auctions (e.g., the English auction) are the most popular auction mechanism. Lucking-Reiley (2000) finds that 85% of the 142 Internet auction sites surveyed in 1998 used an ascending auction format.[8] Fourth, bids are commonly made during the last seconds of an Internet auction that lasts several days or weeks. An interesting hypothesis for this last-minute behavior is that the bidders are tacitly colluding to avoid a bidding war and keep the winning price down.

Within these general auction formats, auctions may have particular characteristics. In English auctions, for example, sellers can set a reserve—a minimum acceptable price that is unobservable to buyers. Greenleaf (2004) argues that behavioral phenomena such as anticipated regret and rejoicing can affect the seller's reserve level. In a related paper, Greenleaf and Sinha (1996) examine buy-in penalties, the amount a seller must pay if the item does not sell. Wang, Montgomery, and Srinivasan (2004) study the "Buy It Now" option on eBay, whereby a seller offers buyers a fixed price up front as an alternative to entering the auction. Using an analytical model and data from eBay, they develop conditions under which such a policy increases the seller's profit and suggest the optimal fixed price.

An interesting question is how to attract customers to an auction (Sinha and Greenleaf 2000). Are there types of people who are attracted to auctions? Do they have different risk profiles than non-auction customers? While more customers are almost always incrementally profitable to a firm using posted prices, more bidders does not necessarily increase actual profits from an auction. How does an auction site optimally allocate resources between bidders and sellers?

Price Search Behavior

The efficiency aspects of the Web are an area of potential research. Is the Web a more efficient environment than its bricks-and-mortar counterpart? Smith, Bailey, and Brynjolfsson (2000) describe four dimensions of Web efficiency: price levels, price elasticity, menu costs, and price dispersion. I discuss each below:

Price Levels   Are the prices charged on the Internet lower? The empirical research comparing online and offline retail price levels is mixed and limited to a few product categories. Bailey (1998) finds that prices for books, CDs, and software are higher on the Internet than in offline stores. Brynjolfsson and Smith (2000) find the reverse: the prices of books and CDs are 9–16% lower on the Internet than in stores. One possibility is that the Internet has become a more efficient place to search for low prices over time in that users have become more familiar with the technology and price search mechanisms have become more sophisticated.

Some work focuses on the implications of the Internet for price competition among firms, both online and offline. Lal and Sarvary (1999) look at the conditions under which the Internet could actually decrease price competition and show that two dimensions—the attribute types of the products in question and the channels being used—can lead to higher prices and less search. Zettelmeyer (2000) relates the size of the Internet (i.e., its reach) to competitive pricing and communications policies.

Price Elasticity Are consumers more sensitive to small price changes on the Internet? Some studies have found that price elasticities on the Web are quite large (Chevalier and Goolsbee 2003). While lower search costs should make it possible for customers to easily collect price information, it could also lower the cost of collecting information about product quality. Some research has found that lowering the search costs for quality for differentiated products (e.g., wine) decreases price sensitivity (Lynch and Ariely 2000), although when an automated "smart" agent is used, price sensitivity can be increased (Diehl, Kornish, and Lynch 2003).

An interesting finding in this context is that customers do not really search that much on the Web. Johnson et al. (2004) analyze Web buying behavior for CDs, books, and air travel services, and find that, on average, households visit only 1.2 books sites, 1.3 CD sites, and 1.8 travel sites during an active month in each category. Thus, it is possible that online price sensitivity could ultimately be lower than offline. Several other studies note that price elasticity is lower in online than offline markets (Degeratu, Rangaswamy, and Wu 2000; Goolsbee 2000).

How does the proliferation of price search engines (price shopbots) affect consumer behavior on the Web? Although not widely used (Montgomery et al. 2003), clearly, price search engines reduce search costs even more and focus exclusively on price. A study by Ellison and Ellison (2004) shows that for electronics products, price elasticities can be very large when prices are searched using a shopbot. Interestingly, although the shopbots focus exclusively on price and rank-order retailers by the price of the searched product, Smith and Brynjolfsson (2001) find that the retailer brand is still important, in that customers use the brand name as a proxy for the retailer's credibility on nonproduct dimensions of the offering, such as shipping time.

Menu Costs Do retailers adjust their prices more finely or frequently on the Internet? Bailey (1998) finds that menu costs on the Internet are lower than in offline retailing, in that the Internet merchants make significantly more price changes than their offline counterparts. Brynjolfsson and Smith (2000) test the menu cost hypothesis by examining whether Internet retailers make smaller price changes, which

would be prevented by higher menu costs. They find that the smallest
Internet price change for books is $.05 while it is $.35 for offline stores;
for CDs, the smallest Internet price change is $.01 while it is $1.00 for
conventional stores.

Price Dispersion   Is there a smaller spread between the highest and
lowest prices on the Internet? Ease of entry on the Internet should create more competition and, along with lower search costs, should reduce
price dispersion as prices converge on a single competitive price. This is
shown empirically for online bookstores (Clay, Krishnan, and Wolff
2001). On the other hand, price dispersion could also exist on the
Internet due to differential search costs and information levels across
customers and due to website/brand differentiation. (Some of this differentiation may come from lock-in strategies such as Amazon's one-
click ordering system.) Comparing Amazon.com and Barnes & Noble's
online sites, Chevalier and Goolsbee (2003) find that, in fact, online
price dispersion is greater online than offline. In a survey of a number of
empirical studies, Pan, Ratchford, and Shankar (2004) conclude (1)
there is substantial price dispersion on the Internet, and (2) there is no
evidence that there is less price variation on the Internet than in offline
environments. In addition, a longitudinal analysis shows that while the
dispersion on the Internet has declined slightly over time, it is still substantial. Another source of online price dispersion may be "hit-and-run"
promotional pricing (Baye, Morgan, and Scholten 2004).

Directions for Future Research

While there has been a considerable amount of research on pricing, there is a lot that we still do not know. An overarching issue is that virtually all of the work cited in this monograph has been conducted in consumer markets. We know fairly little about how these results translate to business-to-business markets. Price is, and should continue to be, the marketing mix variable that economists and marketing academics study most often.

My comments about future areas of research are summarized by topic area.

Customer Value: Measurement and Scaling Issues

Except for the several studies described in this paper, issues related to measuring and scaling customer value (or willingness-to-pay) have not been extensively studied since the 1970s. This is a very important, practical area in which marketing academics can have a large impact. In today's price-sensitive market, understanding price thresholds and willingness-to-pay is critical to marketing managers' ability to price appropriately and not succumb to extreme pressure to drop prices if a competitor does so. Managers still lack an easy-to-use approach to measuring WTP over market segments and in a variety of situations; critical future research could be conducted in this area. In general, the entire area of price responsiveness needs further work, particularly with respect to how the Internet has affected price responsiveness.

Behavioral Response to Price

Measurement research can help managers set prices, but we also need to study how customers are utilizing price information to make decisions. Fortunately, a substantial body of knowledge has been accumulated in some behavioral areas. We have developed a fairly good idea of how much knowledge consumers have about prices, and the literature on reference price is expansive and comprehensive. However, more work is needed to better understand customers' reactions to and processing of price information, particularly in this era of dynamic prices with an increasing number of price tactics. New methods of measuring consumer response to stimuli developed in neuroscience could provide some exciting insights (Camerer, Loewenstein, and Prelec 2005). We still know little about the power of "odd" prices and why they are effective in a variety of circumstances. The literature on context effects is increasing, but given the many contexts in which price information is processed, there is room for more work in this area.

Pricing Tactics

Research on pricing tactics will continue to grow as companies create new approaches to pricing their products and services. Academics are often reactive in this area: we attempt to better understand new pricing policies that have been adopted in practice. For example, one area that companies are exploring is hidden price increases: shrinking the package size but retaining the original price. In dynamic pricing research, however, advances in optimization models along with large-scale data processing should lead practice. Finally, research on currency and spare-change effects needs to be expanded to better understand how customers perceive money.

Empirical Research on Price

This has been one of the most heavily studied areas of pricing because most empirical choice models include some measure of price. Given the pace of new methodological developments, we will always have new applications that will make it possible for us to better understand customer and market sensitivities to pricing policies. More research should be conducted using the NEIO approach, which incorporates supply and demand conditions in a competitive environment. A particularly interesting stream of research, which cuts across all domains of price research, utilizes the results of controlled field experiments. More work is needed on the interaction of price and the other marketing mix variables.

Game-Theoretic Models

A considerable amount of work has been done on the implications of price using game-theoretic models with competitive interactions and channels. Since we are moving into a multichannel business world very rapidly, it would be particularly useful if this work were expanded to include such channels as the Internet, wireless devices such as personal digital assistants, and so forth.

Pricing and the Internet

Given the rapid growth of the Internet and e-commerce, we need to better understand appropriate pricing policies and mechanisms for this new distribution channel and communications medium. It is clear that the Internet is attracting both price-sensitive and price-insensitive customers. In addition, pricing policy is inextricably tied to product policy: mass customization, or individually tailored products and services, should imply pricing flexibility. Price experimentation should be easy and inexpensive. However, at this stage in the development of the Internet, we do not know very much about optimal pricing policies or consumers' behavioral aspects except in a very few product categories, such as CDs and books.

Notes

1. For practical purposes, this can be thought of as an average or segment-level concept.
2. Cost is, of course, a complex concept as there are many kinds of costs and cost allocation mechanisms.
3. The terms "customer value," "reservation price," and "willingness-to-pay" are used interchangeably. In all cases, the interpretation is the maximum a customer is willing to pay for a product or service.
4. The Guadagni-Little model is essentially the reference price choice model described earlier without the reference price term(s) (depending on the specification).
5. Whether the interaction effects are asymmetric is an interesting question. It is conventional wisdom that promotion should negatively affect advertising, particularly image/brand equity-oriented advertising. However, it is unclear how advertising spending should affect promotion.
6. If online sales from auctions, tickets, and travel are included, online sales represent 5.5% of all retail sales (Mangalindan 2005).
7. The changes made possible by the Internet are only one manifestation of the impact of information technology on pricing decisionmaking. In the retailing sector, bar codes and the emerging RFID technologies make it possible for retailers to update prices more efficiently from a central database than they were able to using the manual price tag approach.
8. Other research (Fay 2004) has investigated name-your-own-price auctions such as Priceline.

References

Adam, Daniel (1958), "Consumer Reactions to Price." *Observation Economics* 15, 15–21.

Alba, Joseph W., Susan M. Broniarczyk, Terence A. Shimp, and Joel E. Urbany (1994), "The Influence of Prior Beliefs, Frequency Cues, and Magnitude Cues on Consumers' Perceptions of Comparative Price Data." *Journal of Consumer Research* 21 (September), 219–35.

Alba, Joseph, John Lynch, Barton Weitz, Chris Janiszewski, Richard Lutz, Alan Sawyer, and Stacy Wood (1997), "Interactive Home Shopping: Consumer, Retailer, and Manufacturer Incentives to Participate in Electronic Marketplaces." *Journal of Marketing* 61 (July), 38–53.

Alba, Joseph W., Carl F. Mela, Terence A. Shimp, and Joel E. Urbany (1999), "The Effect of Discount Frequency and Depth on Consumer Price Judgments." *Journal of Consumer Research* 26 (September), 99–114.

Albert, Terri, and Russell S. Winer (2005), "Capturing Customers' Spare Change." *Harvard Business Review* 83 (March), 28.

Anderson, Eric T., and Duncan I. Simester (2003), "Effect of $9 Price Endings on Retail Sales: Evidence from Field Experiments." *Quantitative Marketing and Economics* 1 (March), 93–110.

Assmus, Gert, John U. Farley, and Donald R. Lehmann (1984), "How Advertising Affects Sales: Meta-Analysis of Econometric Results." *Journal of Marketing Research* 21 (February), 65–74.

Bailey, Joseph P. (1998), "Intermediation and Electronic Markets: Aggregation and Pricing in Internet Commerce." Cambridge, Mass.: MIT, Unpublished Ph.D. dissertation.

Bajari, Patrick, and Ali Hortaçu (2003), "Cyberspace Auctions and Pricing Issues: A Review of Empirical Findings." In *New Economy Handbook*, ed. Derek C. Jones, Chapter 7. Amsterdam, Netherlands: Elsevier.

Bajari, Patrick, and Ali Hortaçu (2004), "Economic Insights from Internet Auctions." *Journal of Economic Literature* 42 (June), 457–86.

Bakos, Yannis (2001), "The Emerging Landscape for Retail E-Commerce." *Journal of Economic Perspectives* 15 (Winter), 69–80.

Bakos, Yannis, and Erik Brynjolfsson (1999), "Bundling Information Goods: Pricing, Profits and Efficiency." *Management Science* 45 (December), 1613–30.

Bass, Frank M., Trichy V. Krishnan, and Dipak C. Jain (1994), "Why the Bass Model Fits without Decision Variables." *Marketing Science* 13 (Summer), 203–23.

Baye, Michael R., John Morgan, and Patrick Scholten (2004), "Temporal Price Dispersion: Evidence from an Online Consumer Electronics Market." *Journal of Interactive Marketing* 18 (Autumn), 101–15.

Bell, David R., and James M. Lattin (2000), "Looking for Loss Aversion in Scanner Panel Data: The Confounding Effect of Price Response Heterogeneity." *Marketing Science* 19 (Spring), 185–200.

Bolton, Lisa E., Luk Warlop, and Joseph W. Alba (2003), "Consumer Perceptions of Price (Un)Fairness." *Journal of Consumer Research* 29 (March), 474–91.

Briesch, Richard A., Lakshman Krishnamurthi, Tridib Mazumdar, and S. P. Raj (1997), "A Comparative Analysis of Reference Price Models." *Journal of Consumer Research* 24 (September), 202–14.

Bronnenberg, Bart J., and Wilfried R. Vanhonacker (1996), "Limited Choice Sets, Local Price Response and Implied Measures of Price Competition." *Journal of Marketing Research* 33 (May), 163–74.

Bruce, Norris, Ernan Haruvy, and Ram Rao (2004), "Seller Rating, Price, and Default in Online Auctions." *Journal of Interactive Marketing* 18 (Autumn), 37–50.

Brynjolfsson, Erik, and Michael D. Smith (2000), "Frictionless Commerce? A Comparison of Internet and Conventional Retailers." *Management Science* 46 (April), 563–85.

Camerer, Colin, George Loewenstein, and Drazen Prelec (2005), "Neuroeconomics: How Neuroscience Can Inform Economics." *Journal of Economic Literature* 43 (March), 9–64.

Campbell, Margaret C. (1999), "Perceptions of Price Unfairness: Antecedents and Consequences." *Journal of Marketing Research* 36 (May), 187–99.

Chakravarti, Dipankar, Rajan Krish, Pallab Paul, and Joydeep Srivastava (2002), "Partitioned Presentation of Multicomponent Bundle Prices: Evaluation, Choice and Underlying Processing Effects." *Journal of Consumer Psychology* 12, 215–29.

Chang, Kwangpil, S. Siddarth, and Charles B. Weinberg (1999), "The Impact of Heterogeneity in Purchase Timing and Price Responsiveness on Estimates of Sticker Shock Effects." *Marketing Science* 18 (Spring), 178–92.

Chen, Yuxin, and Ganesh Iyer (2002), "Consumer Addressability and Customized Pricing." *Marketing Science* 21 (Spring), 197–208.

Chen, Yuxin, Chakravarthi Narasimhan, and Z. John Zhang (2001), "Consumer Heterogeneity and Competitive Price-Matching Guarantees." *Marketing Science* 20 (Summer), 300–14.

Chen, Yuxin, and K. Sudhir (2004), "When Shopbots Meet Emails: Implications for Price Competition on the Internet." *Quantitative Marketing and Economics* 2 (September), 233–56.

Chevalier, Judith, and Austan Goolsbee (2003), "Measuring Prices and Price Competition Online: Amazon.com and BarnesandNoble.com." *Quantitative Marketing and Economics* 1 (June), 203–22.

Chintagunta, Pradeep K. (2002), "Investigating Category Pricing Behavior at a Retail Chain." *Journal of Marketing Research* 39 (May), 141–54.

Clay, Karen, Ramayya Krishnan, and Eric Wolff (2001), "Prices and Price Dispersion on the Web: Evidence from the Online Book Industry." *Journal of Industrial Economics* 49 (December), 521–39.

Danaher, Peter J. (2002), "Optimal Pricing of New Subscription Services: Analysis of a Market Experiment." *Marketing Science* 21 (Spring), 119–38.

Degeratu, Alexandru M., Arvind Rangaswamy, and Jianan Wu (2000), "Consumer Choice Behavior in Online and Traditional Supermarkets: The Effects of Brand Name, Price, and Other Search Attributes." *International Journal of Research in Marketing* 17 (March), 55–78.

Desai, Preyas S., and Devavrat Purohit (2004), "'Let Me Talk to My Manager': Haggling in a Competitive Environment." *Marketing Science* 23 (Spring), 219–33.

Desiraju, Ramarao, and Steven M. Shugan (1999), "Strategic Service Pricing and Yield Management." *Journal of Marketing* 63 (January), 44–56.

Dhar, Sanjay K., and Stephen J. Hoch (1996), "Price Discrimination Using In-Store Merchandising." *Journal of Marketing* 60 (January), 17–30.

Dickson, Peter R., and Alan G. Sawyer (1990), "The Price Knowledge and Search of Supermarket Shoppers." *Journal of Marketing* 54 (July), 42–53.

Diehl, Kristin, Laura J. Kornish, and John G. Lynch, Jr. (2003), "Smart Agents: When Lower Search Costs for Quality Information Increase Price Sensitivity." *Journal of Consumer Research* 30 (June), 56–71.

Dolan, Robert J., and Youngme Moon (2000), "Pricing and Market Making on the Internet." Boston, Mass.: Harvard Business School case no. 9–500–065.

Drèze, Xavier, and Joseph C. Nunes (2004), "Using Combined-Currency Prices to Lower Consumers' Perceived Cost." *Journal of Marketing Research* 41 (February), 59–72.

Ellison, Glenn, and Sara Fisher Ellison (2004), "Search, Obfuscation, and Price Elasticities on the Internet." Cambridge, Mass.: MIT, Working Paper.

Emery, Fred (1970), "Some Psychological Aspects of Price." In *Pricing Research*, eds. B. Taylor and G. Wills, 98–111. Princeton, N.J.: Brandon/Systems.

Erdem, Tülin, Susumu Imai, and Michael P. Keane (2003), "Brand and Quantity Choice Dynamics Under Price Uncertainty." *Quantitative Marketing and Economics* 1 (March), 5–64.

Erdem, Tülin, Glenn Mayhew, and Baohong Sun (2001), "Understanding Reference-Price Shoppers: A Within- and Cross-Category Analysis." *Journal of Marketing Research* 38 (November), 445–57.

Estelami, Hooman, Donald R. Lehmann, and Alfred C. Holden (2001), "Macro-Economic Determinants of Consumer Price Knowledge: A Meta-Analysis of Four Decades of Research." *International Journal of Research in Marketing* 18 (December), 341–56.

Fay, Scott (2004), "Partial-Repeat-Bidding in the Name-Your-Own-Price Channel." *Marketing Science* 23 (Summer), 407–18.

Fouilhé, Pierre (1960), "Evaluation Subjective des Prix." *Revue Francaise de Sociologie* 1, 163–72.

Gabor, Andre, and C. W. J. Granger (1961), "On the Price Consciousness of Consumers." *Applied Statistics* 10, 170–88.

Gabor, Andre, and C. W. J. Granger (1966), "Price as an Indicator of Quality: Report on an Inquiry." *Economica* 33, 43–70.

Goolsbee, Austan (2000), "In a World without Borders: The Impact of Taxes on Internet Commerce." *Quarterly Journal of Economics* 115 (May), 561–76.

Gourville, John T. (1998), "Pennies-a-Day: The Effect of Temporal Reframing on Transaction Evaluation." *Journal of Consumer Research* 24 (March), 395–408.

Gourville, John T. (1999), "Note on Behavioral Pricing." Harvard Business School case no. 9-599-114.

Green, Paul E., and V. Srinivasan (1990), "Conjoint Analysis in Marketing: New Developments with Implications for Research and Practice." *Journal of Marketing* 54 (October), 3–19.

Greenleaf, Eric A. (1995), "The Impact of Reference Price Effects on the Profitability of Price Promotions." *Marketing Science* 14 (Winter), 82–104.

Greenleaf, Eric A. (2004), "Reserves, Regret, and Rejoicing in Open English Auctions." *Journal of Consumer Research* 31 (September), 264–73.

Greenleaf, Eric A., and Atanu R. Sinha (1996), "Combining Buy-In Penalties with Commissions at Auction Houses." *Management Science* 42 (April), 529–40.

Grewal, Dhruv, Howard Marmorstein, and Arun Sharma (1996), "Communicating Price Information through Semantic Cues: The Moderating Effects of Situation and Discount Size." *Journal of Consumer Research* 23 (September), 148–56.

Guadagni, Peter M., and John D. C. Little (1983), "A Logit Model of Brand Choice Calibrated on Scanner Data." *Marketing Science* 2 (Summer), 203–38.

Haneman, W. Michael (1994), "Valuing the Environment Through Contingent Valuation." *The Journal of Economic Perspectives* 8 (Autumn), 19–43.

Helson, Harry (1964), *Adaptation-Level Theory*. New York, N.Y.: Harper & Row.

Hoch, Stephen J., Byung-Do Kim, Alan L. Montgomery, and Peter E. Rossi (1995), "Determinants of Store-Level Price Elasticity." *Journal of Marketing Research* 32 (February), 17–29.

Hof, Robert D. (2005), "PayPal Spreads Its Wings." *BusinessWeek* (May 23), 105–6.

Huber, Joel, John W. Payne, and Christopher Puto (1982), "Adding Asymmetrically Dominated Alternatives: Violations of Regularity and the Similarity Hypothesis." *Journal of Consumer Research* 9 (June), 90–8.

Hviid, Morten, and Greg Shaffer (1999), "Hassle Costs: The Achilles Heel of Price-Matching Guarantees." *Journal of Economics and Management Strategy* 8 (December), 489–521.

Jain, Sanjay, and Joydeep Srivastava (2000), "An Experimental and Theoretical Analysis of Price-Matching Refund Policies." *Journal of Marketing Research* 37 (August), 351–62.

Janiszewski, Chris, and Marcus Cunha, Jr. (2004), "The Influence of a Price Discount Framing on the Evaluation of a Product Bundle." *Journal of Consumer Research* 30 (March), 534–46.

Janiszewski, Chris, and Donald R. Lichtenstein (1999), "A Range Theory Account of Price Perception." *Journal of Consumer Research* 25 (March), 353–68.

Jedidi, Kamel, and John Zhang (2002), "Augmenting Conjoint Analysis to Estimate Consumer Reservation Price." *Management Science* 48 (October), 1350–68.

Johnson, Eric J., Wendy W. Moe, Peter S. Fader, Steven Bellman, and Gerald L. Lohse (2004), "On the Depth and Dynamics of Online Search Behavior." *Management Science* 50 (March), 299–308.

Kadiyali, Vrinda, Pradeep Chintagunta, and Naufel Vilcassim (2000), "Manufacturer-Retailer Channel Interactions and Implications for Channel Power: An Empirical Investigation of Pricing in a Local Market." *Marketing Science* 19 (Spring), 127–48.

Kahneman, Daniel, and Amos Tversky (1979), "Prospect Theory: An Analysis of Decision Under Risk." *Econometrica* 47 (March), 263–92.

Kalra, Ajay, and Ronald C. Goodstein (1998), "The Impact of Advertising Positioning Strategies on Consumer Price Sensitivity." *Journal of Marketing Research* 35 (May), 210–24.

Kalyanam, Kirthi, and Thomas S. Shively (1998), "Estimating Irregular Pricing Effects: A Stochastic Spline Regression Approach." *Journal of Marketing Research* 35 (February), 16–29.

Kalyanaram, Gurumurthy, and Russell S. Winer (1995), "Empirical Generalizations from Reference Price Research." *Marketing Science* 14 (Summer, part 2 of 2), G161–69.

Kardes, Frank R., Maria L. Cronley, James J. Kellaris, and Steven S. Posavac (2004), "The Role of Selective Information Processing in Price-Quality Inference." *Journal of Consumer Research* 31 (September), 368–74.

Kaul, Anil, and Dick R. Wittink (1995), "Empirical Generalizations about the Impact of Advertising on Price Sensitivity and Price." *Marketing Science* 14 (Summer, part 2 of 2), G151–160.

Kirmani, Amna, and Akshay R. Rao (2000), "No Pain, No Gain: A Critical Review of the Literature on Signaling Unobservable Product Quality." *Journal of Marketing* 64 (April), 66–79.

Koenigsberg, Oded, Eitan Muller, and Naufel J. Vilcassim (2004), "easyJet Airlines: Small, Lean, and with Prices That Increase over Time." New York, N.Y.: Columbia University, Working Paper.

Kopalle, Praveen K., Ambar G. Rao, and Joao L. Assunçaõ (1996), "Asymmetric Reference Price Effects and Dynamic Pricing Policies." *Marketing Science* 15 (Winter), 60–85.

Kopalle, Praveen, and Russell S. Winer (1996), "A Dynamic Model of Reference Price and Expected Quality." *Marketing Letters* 7 (January) 41–52.

Kridel, Donald J., Dale E. Lehman, and Dennis L. Weisman (1993), "Option Value, Telecommunications Demand, and Policy." *Information Economics and Policy* 5 (June), 125–44.

Krishnamurthy, Lakshman, Tridib Mazumdar, and S. P. Raj (1992), "Asymmetric Response to Price in Consumer Brand Choice and Purchase Quantity Decisions." *Journal of Consumer Research* 19 (December), 387–400.

Krishnan, Trichy V., Frank M. Bass, and Dipak C. Jain (1999), "Optimal Pricing Strategy for New Products." *Management Science* 43 (December), 1650–63.

Lal, Rajiv, and Ram Rao (1997), "Supermarket Competition: The Case of Everyday Low Pricing." *Marketing Science* 16 (Winter), 60–80.

Lal, Rajiv, and Miklos Sarvary (1999), "When and How Is the Internet Likely to Decrease Price Competition?" *Marketing Science* 18 (Autumn), 485–503.

Lambrecht, Anja, and Bernd Skiera (2005), "Paying Too Much and Being Happy About It: Existence, Causes and Consequences of Tariff-Choice Biases." Frankfurt am Main, Germany: Johann Wolfgang Goethe-University, Working Paper.

Leavitt, Harold J. (1954), "A Note on Some Experimental Findings about the Meaning of Price." *Journal of Business* 27 (July), 205–10.

Lee, Eunkyu, and Richard Staelin (1997), "Vertical Strategic Interaction: Implications for Channel Pricing Strategy." *Marketing Science* 16 (Summer), 185–207.

Lucking-Reiley, David (1999), "Using Field Experiments to Test Equivalence Between Auction Formats: Magic on the Internet." *American Economic Review* 89 (December), 1063–80.

Lucking-Reiley, David (2000), "Auctions on the Internet: What's Being Auctioned, and How?" *Journal of Industrial Economics* 48 (September), 227–52.

Lynch, John G., and Dan Ariely (2000), "Wine Online: Search Costs Affect Competition on Price, Quality, and Distribution." *Marketing Science* 19 (Winter), 83–103.

Mangalindan, Mylene (2005), "Online Retail Sales Are Expected to Rise to $172 Billion This Year." *Wall Street Journal* (May 24), D5.

Marbeau, Yves (1987), "What Value Pricing Research Today?" *Journal of the Market Research Society* 29, 153–82.

Marshall, Alfred (1890), *Principles of Economics*. London, U.K.: Macmillan.

Mayhew, Glenn E., and Russell S. Winer (1992), "An Empirical Analysis of Internal and External Reference Price Effects Using Scanner Data." *Journal of Consumer Research* 19 (June), 62–70.

Mazumdar, Tridib, and Purushottam Papatla (2000), "An Investigation of Reference Price Segments." *Journal of Marketing Research* 37 (May), 246–58.

Mela, Carl F., Sunil Gupta, and Donald R. Lehmann (1997), "The Long-Term Impact of Promotion and Advertising on Consumer Brand Choice." *Journal of Marketing Research* 34 (May), 248–61.

Meyvis, Tom, and Jinhong Xie (2005), "Switching between Pricing Schedules: A Dynamic Advantage for Flat Rates." New York, N.Y.: New York University, Stern School of Business, Working Paper.

Mitra, Anusree, and John G. Lynch, Jr. (1995),"Toward a Reconciliation of Market Power and Information Theories of Advertising Effects on Price Elasticity." *Journal of Consumer Research* 21 (March), 644–59.

Monroe, Kent B. (1971a), "Measuring Price Thresholds by Psychophysics and Latitudes of Acceptance." *Journal of Marketing Research* 8 (November), 460–4.

Monroe, Kent B. (1971b), "The Information Content of Prices: A Preliminary Model for Estimating Buyer Response." *Management Science* 17 (April), B519–32.

Monroe, Kent B. (1976), "The Influence of Price Differences and Brand Familiarity on Brand Preferences." *Journal of Consumer Research* 3 (June), 42–9.

Monroe, Kent B. (1990), *Pricing: Making Profitable Decisions*, 2nd ed. New York, N.Y.: McGraw-Hill.

Montgomery, Alan L. (1997), "Creating Micro-Marketing Pricing Strategies Using Supermarket Scanner Data." *Marketing Science* 4 (Autumn), 315–37.

Montgomery, Alan L. (2004), "The Implementation Challenge of Pricing Decision Support Systems for Retail Managers." Pittsburgh, Penn.: Carnegie Mellon University, Working Paper.

Montgomery, Alan L., Kartik Hosanagar, Ramayya Krishnan, and Karen B. Clay (2003), "Designing a Better Shopbot." Pittsburgh, Penn.: Carnegie Mellon University, Working Paper.

Montgomery, Alan L., and Peter E. Rossi (1999), "Estimating Price Elasticities with Theory-Based Priors." *Journal of Marketing Research* 36 (November), 413–23.

Morwitz, Vicki G., Eric A. Greenleaf, and Eric J. Johnson (1998), "Divide and Prosper: Consumers' Reactions to Partitioned Prices." *Journal of Marketing Research* 35 (November), 453–63.

Naik, Prasad A., Kalyan Raman, and Russell S. Winer (2005), "Planning Marketing-Mix Strategies in the Presence of Interaction Effects: Empirical and Equilibrium Analysis." *Marketing Science* 24 (Winter), 25–34.

Narasimhan, Chakravarthi, Scott A. Neslin, and Subrata K. Sen (1996), "Promotional Elasticities and Category Characteristics." *Journal of Marketing* 60 (April), 17–30.

Neslin, Scott A. (2002), *Sales Promotion*. Cambridge, Mass.: Marketing Science Institute.

Nunes, Joseph C. (2000), "A Cognitive Model of People's Usage Estimations." *Journal of Marketing Research* 37 (November), 397–409.

Ofir, Chezy (2004), "Reexamining Latitude of Price Acceptability and Price Thresholds: Predicting Basic Consumer Reaction to Price." *Journal of Consumer Research* 30 (March), 612–21.

Ofir, Chezy, Gordon G. Bechtel, and Russell S. Winer (2000), "Price Acceptability Thresholds: A Thurstonian Approach." Jerusalem, Israel: The Hebrew University, Working Paper.

Pan, Xing, Brian T. Ratchford, and Venkatesh Shankar (2004), "Price Dispersion on the Internet: A Review and Directions for Future Research." *Journal of Interactive Marketing* 18 (Autumn), 116–35.

Posavac, Steven S. (2001), "Overbidding in Value Elicitation: When Consumers Report Inflated Reservation Prices, and What to Do About It." *Journal of Consumer Psychology* 11, 87–97.

Prelec, Drazen, and Duncan Simester (2001), "Always Leave Home without It: A Further Investigation of the Credit-Card Effect on Willingness to Pay." *Marketing Letters* 12 (February), 5–12.

Raghubir, Priya (1998), "Coupon Value: A Signal for Price?" *Journal of Marketing Research* 35 (August), 316–24.

Raghubir, Priya, and Joydeep Srivastava (2002), "Effect of Face Value on Product Valuation in Foreign Currencies." *Journal of Consumer Research* 29 (December), 335–47.

Raghubir, Priya, and Joydeep Srivastava (2004), "The Denomination Effect." Berkeley, Calif.: University of California at Berkeley, Working Paper.

Rajendran, K. N., and Gerard J. Tellis (1994), "Contextual and Temporal Components of Reference Price." *Journal of Marketing* 58 (January), 22–34.

Raju, Jagmohan, and Z. John Zhang (2005), "Channel Coordination in the Presence of a Dominant Retailer." *Marketing Science* 24 (Spring), 254–62.

Rao, Akshay R., Mark Bergen, and Scott Davis (2000), "How to Fight a Price War." *Harvard Business Review* 78 (February), 107–16.

Rao, Akshay R., and Kent B. Monroe (1989), "The Effect of Price, Brand Name, and Store Name on Buyers' Perceptions of Product Quality: An Integrative Review." *Journal of Marketing Research* 26 (August), 351–7.

Schindler, Robert M., and Patrick N. Kirby (1997), "Patterns of Rightmost Digits Used in Advertised Prices: Implications for Nine-Ending Effects." *Journal of Consumer Research* 24 (September), 192–201.

Scitovsky, Tibor (1944–45), "Some Consequences of the Habit of Judging Quality by Price." *Review of Economic Studies* 12, 100.

Scott Morton, Fiona, Florian Zettelmeyer, and Jorge Silva-Russo (2003), "Consumer Information and Discrimination: Does the Internet Affect the Pricing of New Cars to Women and Minorities?" *Quantitative Marketing and Economics* 1 (March), 65–92.

Scott Morton, Fiona, Florian Zettelmeyer, and Jorge Silva-Russo (2001), "Internet Car Retailing." *The Journal of Industrial Economics* 49 (December), 501–19.

Scott Morton, Fiona, Florian Zettelmeyer, and Jorge Silva-Russo (2005), "How the Internet Lowers Prices: Evidence from Matched Survey and Auto Transaction Data." Berkeley, Calif.: University of California, Berkeley, Working Paper.

Sherif, Muzafer, and Carol Hovland (1953), "Judgmental Phenomena and Scales of Attitude Measurement: Placement of Items with Individual Choice of Number of Categories." *Journal of Abnormal and Social Psychology* 48 (January), 135–41.

Simonson, Itamar, and Aimee Drolet (2004), "Anchoring Effects on Consumers' Willingness-to-Pay and Willingness-to-Accept." *Journal of Consumer Research* 31 (December), 681–90.

Sinha, Atanu R., and Eric A. Greenleaf (2000), "Valuing and Attracting Bidders and Sellers: Traditional Auctions and the Internet." New York, N.Y.: New York University, Stern School of Business, Working Paper.

Smith, Michael D., Joseph Bailey, and Erik Brynjolfsson (2000), "Understanding Digital Markets: Review and Assessment." In *Understanding the Digital Economy*, eds. Erik Brynjolfsson and Brian Kahin, 99–136. Cambridge, Mass.: MIT Press.

Smith, Michael D., and Erik Brynjolfsson (2001), "Consumer Decision-making at an Internet Shopbot: Brand Still Matters." *Journal of Industrial Economics* 49 (December), 541–58.

Soman, Dilip, and John T. Gourville (2001), "Transaction Decoupling: How Price Bundling Affects the Decision to Consume." *Journal of Marketing Research* 37 (February), 30–44.

Spann, Martin, Bernd Skiera, and Björn Schäfers (2004), "Measuring Individual Frictional Costs and Willingness-to-Pay via Name-Your-Own-Price Mechanisms." *Journal of Interactive Marketing* 18 (Autumn), 22–36.

Srivastava, Joydeep, Dipankar Chakravarti, and Amnon Rapoport (2000), "Price and Margin Negotiations in Marketing Channels: An Experimental Study of Sequential Bargaining under One-Sided Uncertainty and Opportunity Cost of Delay." *Marketing Science* 19 (Spring), 163–85.

Srivastava, Joydeep, and Nicholas Lurie (2001), "A Consumer Perspective on Price-Matching Refund Policies: Effect on Price Perceptions and Search Behavior." *Journal of Consumer Research* 28 (September), 296–307.

Stigler, George J. (1961), "The Economics of Information." *The Journal of Political Economy*, 69 (June), 213–25.

Stiving, Mark, and Russell S. Winer (1997), "An Empirical Analysis of Price Endings with Scanner Data." *Journal of Consumer Research* 24 (June), 57–68.

Stoetzel, Jean (1970), "Psychological/Sociological Aspects of Price." In *Pricing Strategy*, eds. Bernard Taylor and Gordon Wills, 70–4. Princeton, N.J.: Brandon/Systems.

Stoetzel, Jean, Jacque Sauerwein, and Alain de Vulpian (1954), "Reflections: French Research: Consumer Studies." In *La Psychologie Economique*, ed. P. L. Reynaud, 183–8. Paris, France: Librairie Marcel Riviere et Cie.

Stremersch, Stefan, and Gerard J. Tellis (2002), "Strategic Bundling of Products and Prices: A New Synthesis for Marketing." *Journal of Marketing* 66 (January), 55–72.

Sudhir, K. (2001), "Competitive Pricing Behavior in the Auto Market: A Structural Analysis." *Marketing Science* 20 (Winter), 42–60.

Swait, Joffre, Tülin Erdem, Jordan Louviere, and Chris Dubelaar (1993), "The Equalization Price: A Measure of Consumer-Perceived Brand Equity." *International Journal of Research in Marketing* 10 (March), 23–45.

Szabo, Nick (1999), "Micropayments and Mental Transaction Costs." Available at www.best.com/~szabo.

Tellis, Gerard J. (1988), "The Price Elasticity of Selective Demand: A Meta-Analysis of Econometric Models of Sales." *Journal of Marketing Research* 25 (November), 331–41.

Thaler, Richard H. (1985), "Mental Accounting and Consumer Choice." *Marketing Science* 4 (Summer), 199–214.

Thomas, Manoj, and Vicki Morwitz (2005), "Penny Wise and Pound Foolish: The Left-Digit Effect in Price Cognition." *Journal of Consumer Research* 32 (June) 54–64.

Thurstone, L. L. (1927), "A Law of Comparative Judgment." *Psychological Review* 34, 273–86.

Train, Kenneth E. (1991), *Optimal Regulation: The Economic Theory of Natural Monopoly*. Cambridge, Mass.: MIT Press.

Urbany, Joel E., Peter R. Dickson, and Rosemary Kalapurakal (1996), "Price Search in the Retail Grocery Market." *Journal of Marketing* 60 (April), 91–104.

U.S. Census Bureau (2005), "Quarterly Retail E-Commerce Sales Report, 1st Quarter 2005." http://www.census.gov/mrts/www/data/html/05Q1.html.

Vandenbosch, Mark B., and Charles B. Weinberg (1995), "Product and Price Competition in a Two-dimensional Vertical Differentiation Model." *Marketing Science* 2 (Spring), 224–9.

Vanhuele, Marc, and Xavier Drèze (2002), "Measuring the Price Knowledge Shoppers Bring to the Store." *Journal of Marketing* 66 (October), 72–85.

Van Westendorp, P. (1976), "NSS-Price Sensitivity Meter: A New Approach to the Study of Consumer Perception of Prices." ESOMAR Congress, 139–67.

Venkatesh, R., and Vijay Mahajan (1997), "Products with Branded Components: An Approach for Premium Pricing and Partner Selection." *Marketing Science* 16 (Spring), 146–65.

Vickrey, William (1961), "Counterspeculation, Auctions, and Competitive Sealed Tenders." *Journal of Finance* 16 (May), 302–14.

Wallsten, Thomas S., David V. Budescu, Amnon Rappaport, Rami Zwick, and Barbara Forsyth (1986), "Measuring the Vague Meaning of Probability Terms." *Journal of Experimental Psychology: General* 115, 348–65.

Wang, Xin, Alan L. Montgomery, and Kannan Srinivasan (2004), "When Auction Meets Fixed Price: A Theoretical and Empirical Examination of Buy-It-Now Auctions." Pittsburgh, Penn.: Carnegie Mellon University, Working Paper.

Wertenbroch, Klaus, and Bernd Skiera (2002), "Measuring Consumers' Willingness to Pay at the Point of Purchase." *Journal of Marketing Research* 39 (May), 228–41.

Winer, Russell S. (1985), "A Price Vector Model of Demand for Consumer Durables: Preliminary Developments." *Marketing Science* 4 (Winter), 74–90.

Winer, Russell S. (1986), "A Reference Price Model of Brand Choice for Frequently Purchased Products." *Journal of Consumer Research* 13 (September), 250–6.

Winer, Russell S. (1988), "Behavioral Perspectives on Pricing: Buyers' Subjective Perceptions of Price Revisited." In *Issues in Pricing: Theory and Research*, ed. Timothy Devinney, 35–57. Lexington, Mass.: Lexington Books.

Xia, Lan, Kent B. Monroe, and Jennifer L. Cox (2004), "The Price Is Unfair! A Conceptual Framework of Price Fairness Perceptions." *Journal of Marketing* 68 (October), 1–15.

Yadav, Manjit S. (1994), "How Buyers Evaluate Product Bundles: A Model of Anchoring and Adjustment." *Journal of Consumer Research* 21 (September), 342–54.

Zettelmeyer, Florian (2000), "Expanding to the Internet: Pricing and Communications Strategies When Firms Compete on Multiple Channels." *Journal of Marketing Research* 37 (August), 292–308.

ABOUT THE AUTHOR

Russell S. Winer is the Deputy Dean and William Joyce Professor of Marketing at the Stern School of Business, New York University. He received a B.A. in economics from Union College and an M.S. and Ph.D. in industrial administration from Carnegie Mellon University. He has been on the faculties of Columbia and Vanderbilt universities and, most recently, the University of California at Berkeley. He has been a visiting faculty member at MIT, Stanford University, Cranfield School of Management (United Kingdom), the Helsinki School of Economics, the University of Tokyo, and École Nationale des Ponts et Chausées at a number of their campuses, including those in Paris, Casablanca, Buenos Aires, and Cochin, India.

He has written three books, *Marketing Management, Analysis for Marketing Planning,* and *Product Management,* and has authored over 60 papers in marketing on a variety of topics, including consumer choice, marketing research methodology, marketing planning, advertising, and pricing. He is particularly well-known for his research incorporating psychological concepts of price into brand choice models.

He is a past editor of the *Journal of Marketing Research* and the *Journal of Interactive Marketing,* and is on the editorial boards of the *Journal of Marketing,* the *Journal of Marketing Research,* and *Marketing Science.* He has participated in executive education programs around the world, and is currently an advisor to a number of startup companies.

ABOUT MSI

The Marketing Science Institute connects businesspeople and academic researchers who are committed to advancing the theory and practice of marketing in order to achieve higher levels of business performance. Founded in 1961, MSI currently brings together executives from approximately 65 sponsoring corporations with leading researchers from over 100 universities worldwide.

As a nonprofit institution, MSI financially supports academic research for the development—and practical translation—of leading-edge marketing knowledge on topics of importance to business. Issues of key importance to business performance are identified by the Board of Trustees, which represents MSI corporations and the academic community. MSI supports studies by academics on these issues and disseminates the results through conferences and workshops, as well as through its publications series.

Related MSI Working Papers

Report No.

04-113 "The Effect of Retailer Reputation and Response on Postpurchase Consumer Reactions to Price-Matching Guarantees" by Hooman Estelami, Dhruv Grewal, and Anne L. Roggeveen

03-124 "Adoption and Effectiveness of Loyalty Programs: The Retailer's Perspective" by Jorna Leenheer and Tammo H.A. Bijmolt

03-117 "Minimum Prices and Product Valuations in Auctions" by Gerald Häubl and Peter T. L. Popkowski Leszczyc

03-110 "Long-term Performance Impact of New Products and Promotions in the Auto Industry" by Koen Pauwels, Jorge Silva-Risso, Shuba Srinivasan, and Dominique M. Hanssens

02-116 "The Brand Switching Fraction of Promotion Effects: Unit Sales versus Elasticity Decompositions" by Harald J. van Heerde, Sachin Gupta, and Dick R. Wittink

02-109 "The Effect of Store Brand Share on Retail Margins: An Empirical Analysis" by Kusum L. Ailawadi and Bari A. Harlam

02-107 "Flexible Decomposition of Price Promotion Effects Using Store-level Scanner Data" by Harald J. van Heerde, Peter S.H. Leeflang, and Dick Wittink

01-120 "Do Promotions Benefit Manufacturers, Retailers, or Both?" by Shuba Srinivasan, Koen Pauwels, Dominique Hanssens, and Marnik Dekimpe

01-118 "The Impact of Business Objectives and the Time Horizon of Performance Evaluation on Pricing Behavior" by Sev K. Keil, David Reibstein, and Dick R. Wittink

01-117 "Pricing Process as a Capability: A Case Study" by Shantanu Dutta, Mark Zbaracki, and Mark Bergen

92-107 "A Model Incorporating Promotion Signal Sensitivity for Prescribing Retailer Promotion Policy" by J. Jeffrey Inman and Leigh McAlister

92-105 "Promotion Has a Negative Effect on Brand Evaluations—Or Does It? Additional Disconfirming Evidence" by Scott Davis, Jeffrey Inman, and Leigh McAlister

92-103 "Conference on Sales Promotions from the Consumer, Manufacturer, and Retailer Perspectives" conference summary by George Low

91-130 "Price and Brand Name as Indicators of Quality Dimensions" by Merrie Brucks and Valarie A. Zeithaml

91-106 "Modeling Competitive Pricing and Market Share: Anatomy of a Decision Support System" by Paul E. Green and Abba M. Krieger

90-112 "Consumer Knowledge of Normal Prices: An Exploratory Study and Framework" by Joel E. Urbany and Peter R. Dickson

90-109 "Analyzing Variations in Advertising and Promotional Expenditures: Key Correlates in Consumer, Industrial, and Service Markets" by Siva K. Balasubramanian and V. Kumar